FOR MY DAUGHTER, LORI

Written by Dr Maggie Aderin-Pocock
Illustrated by Chelen Écija

Edited by Frances Evans

Designed by Zoe Bradley

Cover design by John Bigwood

Fact-checking by Stuart Atkinson

Additional illustrations by Jade Moore

First published in Great Britain in 2022 by Buster Books,
9 Lion Yard, Tremadoc Road, London SW4 7NQ

W www.mombooks.com/buster
F Buster Books
T @BusterBooks
I @buster_books

Text © Dr Maggie Aderin-Pocock 2022
Illustrations and layouts © Buster Books 2022

All rights reserved. No part of this book may be reproduced, stored in a retrieval system, or transmitted in any form or by any means, without the prior permission in writing of the publisher, nor be otherwise circulated in any form of binding or cover other than that in which it is published and without a similar condition including this condition being imposed on the subsequent purchaser.

A CIP catalogue record for this book is available from the British Library.

ISBN: 978-1-78055-754-0

2 4 6 8 10 9 7 5 3 1

This book was printed in July 2022 by Leo Paper Products Ltd, Heshan Astros Printing Limited, Xuantan Temple Industrial Zone, Gulao Town, Heshan City, Guangdong Province, China.

CONTENTS

INTRODUCING DR MAGGIE   4
How this book works   5

CHAPTER 1: THE UNIVERSE   6
Did the Universe really begin with a 'Big Bang'?   8
How big is the Universe?   10
Quick questions on … stars   12
Am I made of stardust?   14
Can a star turn into a planet?   16
Why are planets round?   17
What is a black hole?   18
What would happen if I fell into a black hole?   20
What are the colourful clouds in space made of?   22
Are there other planets like ours?   24
Does life exist on other planets?   26
What do aliens look like?   28
What is the 'Milky Way'?   30
Are there other galaxies?   31
How will the Universe end?   32

CHAPTER 2: OUR SOLAR SYSTEM   34
How big is the Sun?   36
How close could a spaceship get to the Sun before it melted?   38
Why isn't Mercury the hottest planet?   40
Can I see any planets in the night sky from Earth?   42
Quick questions on … moons   44
Is there night and day on the Moon?   46
Why don't people walk upside down on the bottom of Earth?   48
Has there ever been life on Mars?   50
How do you land a spaceship on Mars?   52
How many rovers have been to Mars?   54
Could I land on a comet?   56
Does it really rain diamonds on Jupiter?   58
What is Jupiter's 'Great Red Spot'?   60
Could I slide around Saturn's rings?   62
Why is Uranus on its side?   64
What makes Neptune blue?   66
Is Pluto a planet?   68
Are there other dwarf planets?   69
Quick questions on … shooting stars   70
Why is gravity different on other planets?   72
What is an eclipse?   74
Can you see solar eclipses on other planets?   76
Are there rainbows on other planets?   78

CHAPTER 3: HUMANS IN SPACE   80
What happens during lift-off?   82
Why do astronauts float inside spaceships?   84
How do astronauts breathe inside spaceships?   86
Why do astronauts wear spacesuits?   88
What does it feel like to go on a spacewalk?   90
What does space smell like?   92
Quick questions on … life on the ISS   94
Why don't we live on other planets yet?   96
Could we grow plants on other planets?   98
Could animals come and live with us on other planets?   100
Could I sing in space?   102
Could I use my phone in space?   104
How do I become an astronaut?   106
Quick questions on … space records   108
Did a person drive a car on the Moon?   110
How far can space telescopes see?   112
What's the furthest object from Earth that a spacecraft has landed on?   113
Will everyone be travelling into space 100 years from now?   114

Glossary   116
Index   118
Picture credits   120

INTRODUCING DR MAGGIE

Hello! My name is Dr Maggie. I am a space scientist and I have a life-long passion for sharing the wonders of space and science with readers like you. Most of all, I love answering your questions about the Universe. In this book, I've collected some of my all-time favourite questions, from 'What would happen if I fell into a black hole?' to 'Could animals come and live with us on other planets?' I hope you enjoy reading them as much as I've enjoyed answering them.

Maggie Aderin-Pocock

HOW THIS BOOK WORKS

You can open this book on any question you like – you don't have to read them in a particular order. But to help keep similar topics together, I've grouped the questions into three chapters.

In **chapter 1**, we look at some of the BIG stuff – black holes, nebulae, the Big Bang – and explore the distant reaches of the Universe.

In **chapter 2**, we get closer to home and take a tour around our fascinating Solar System.

In **chapter 3**, we look at human space exploration and what the future might hold for our travels into the cosmos.

You'll see me popping up throughout the book. I'm also joined by my robot assistant, IQ ('IQ' stands for 'Interesting Question'!), who will be on hand to help me unpack the science behind the questions.

Finally, you'll find a glossary at the back of the book where useful words and terms are explained.

KEEP AN EYE OUT FOR ...

 **'Try This At Home' activities** – these are hands-on things you can do at home to explore some of the questions further.

 Astro Facts – these are fun, extra bits of information that relate to the topic we're looking at on the page.

CHAPTER 1: THE UNIVERSE

The Universe is EVERYTHING. It's the word we use to describe all of space and everything in it, from galaxies and nebulae to black holes and stars. Our Earth is just a teeny, tiny part of this immense cosmic system. In this chapter, we're going to zoom right out to the distant reaches of the Universe, exploring how it formed and getting up close to some of its strangest phenomena.

DID THE UNIVERSE REALLY BEGIN WITH A 'BIG BANG'?

There are different theories about how the Universe began. But the theory that works best with what we can see out there is called the 'Big Bang' theory. The idea came out of the work of an American astronomer called Edwin Hubble. In the 1920s, Hubble used the biggest telescope available at the time to look deep into space.

SPECIAL STARS

Hubble started looking at a type of star called a Cepheid variable. These stars are unusual because their light dims and brightens over a period of days. The speed at which the stars go from bright to dim tells us how truly bright the star is. If we know how bright the star is, we can work out how far away it is.

Hubble discovered that many of the stars he could see were really far away. Some were in other galaxies altogether. This was a shock because, at the time, people thought our galaxy was the only one in the Universe.

SCIENTISTS THINK THAT THE UNIVERSE IS 13.8 BILLION YEARS OLD. THAT'S A LOT OF BIRTHDAYS!

TURN BACK TIME

Hubble noticed that most stars and galaxies were moving away from Earth. If things were moving away from us now, this meant that, in the past, everything in the Universe was closer together. And if you went back to the beginning, the whole Universe would be squished up in a teeny, tiny speck.

The idea is that this speck suddenly expanded in an event called the 'Big Bang'. This expansion created all the space, time and energy that we know as the 'Universe'.

Try This At Home

Take a deflated balloon and draw stars on it with a felt-tip pen. Start to blow up the balloon and notice that the stars begin to move away from each other. This is similar to how objects move away from one another as the Universe expands. If you let the air out of the balloon, it is like you are turning back time. As you do this, you can see the stars coming together.

HOW BIG IS THE UNIVERSE?

We don't know for certain how big the Universe is. It may stretch on forever. But we can measure the part of the Universe that we can see from Earth. This is called the 'observable Universe'.

ANCIENT LIGHT

We know that the Universe was formed roughly 13.8 billion years ago and probably began with the Big Bang (pages 8–9). Because light takes time to get to us, we can only see light that has been travelling for 13.8 billion years in our direction. You can think of the observable Universe like a ginormous bubble around Earth that stretches for 13.8 billion light years in each direction, or 27.6 billion light years across. To put this in perspective, one light year is the distance that light travels in one year, which is nearly 10 trillion km. Light is super fast!

THIS MAP SHOWS THE RADIATION IN THE UNIVERSE LEFT OVER FROM THE BIG BANG.

EXPANDING UNIVERSE

The problem with this measurement is that the Universe has been expanding since the Big Bang took place. This means that an object whose light we see today at the edge of the observable Universe is even further away now than when the light first left it.

Once we take this expansion into account, the observable Universe gets EVEN bigger, stretching 46.5 billion light years from Earth or 92 billion light years across. It's hard to picture just how enormous this is, but if you imagine the observable Universe as a sports stadium, our planet would be a microscopic speck of bacteria on the floor.

Astro Fact

The edge of the observable Universe isn't the end of the Universe itself. We don't know what lies beyond the observable Universe because the light hasn't reached us yet, so we can't see it. But it could stretch on and on and on and on ...

QUICK QUESTIONS ON ...
STARS

WHERE DO STARS COME FROM?

A star is created inside clouds of dust and gas called nebulae (pages 22–23). Nebulae are usually cold and stable, but if they are disturbed, the material inside can start to clump together due to gravity. This can cause the nebula to collapse and, as this happens, material in the middle of it begins to heat up. This hot core gathers more dust and gas around it. If the core gets hot enough for fusion (page 14) to take place, a new star will be born.

COULD I TOUCH A STAR?

Stars are big balls of gas, so they don't have a solid surface that you could touch. Even if you could get close to one, you wouldn't want to stay there for long – stars are hot. The core of our closest star, the Sun, is 15 million °C! That's 55,000 times hotter than the highest temperature on your kitchen oven.

WHERE DO STARS GO DURING THE DAY?

The stars you can see at night are still there during the day – you just can't see them because the sky is so bright. During the day, we are facing in the direction of the Sun – it is the closest star to Earth and the brightest object in our sky. At night, we face away from the Sun, so the sky is dark and we can see all the other stars.

HOW LONG WOULD IT TAKE TO FLY TO OUR NEAREST STARS?

The Sun is the nearest star to us on Earth, but it is still a long way away – an average of 149 million km. A rocket travelling at the speed of the International Space Station (28,000 km per hour) would take 222 days – nearly 8 months – to get there.

After the Sun, our next closest star is Proxima Centauri, which is about 40 trillion km away. Even if we used the fastest space technology available at the moment, which is around 17 km per second, it would take 76,000 years to arrive there.

AM I MADE OF STARDUST?

The answer to this question is a wonderful 'Yes'! Each and every one of us is made of stardust. Not only that, the pages of this book are made of stardust, as is the chair you're sitting on and the floor your feet are touching. Almost everything in the Universe first came from a star. To explain how, we need to look inside the heart of one.

FUSION

In the centre of every star a process called fusion is taking place. This happens due to the huge pressures and temperatures that exist in a star's centre. Under these conditions, the elements that make up the star are squeezed together so much that they make new elements. These include oxygen, carbon and iron — elements that are found in human bodies. The bigger the star, the more elements are created. Towards the end of a star's life, the elements inside it form layers.

O = OXYGEN   SI = SILICON   FE = IRON

THE LAYERS INSIDE A LARGE STAR

OUT WITH A BANG

So how do the elements at the heart of a star end up in our bodies? The short answer is that they are let loose during the death of a star.

Like animals, stars have a life cycle – they are born, they live and they die. During a star's life, there is a balance between the force of gravity pulling in and the forces generated by fusion pushing out.

Eventually, the star runs out of the fuel it needs for fusion to take place. When this happens to a very large star, gravity takes over and the star starts to collapse very quickly. This causes a spike in pressure and temperature, which allows the star to make heavier elements, such as gold and silver. After this, the star explodes in an event called a supernova. BOOM!

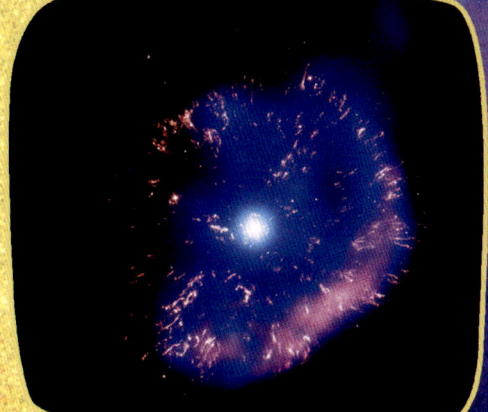

AN EXPLODED STAR

STARS IN YOUR EYES

When a supernova happens, all the elements that have been made in the star's heart shoot out into space. The elements sit in clouds of dust and gas that form into new stars. These new stars go through the same cycle as the original star, and when they die, they release more elements out into space.

Over billions of years, these elements combined to make other things, such as gases and minerals, which in turn made bigger things, such as planets, water and other ingredients required for life. And, eventually, they came together to make us!

CAN A STAR TURN INTO A PLANET?

Sort of. There are objects in space called 'brown dwarfs' that sit somewhere between stars and planets. A brown dwarf goes through some unusual changes in its life, which sees it transform from a sort-of star into a sort-of planet.

To understand how this happens, we need to look at the differences between a star and a planet. A star creates its own energy in the form of light and radiation thanks to the process of fusion (page 14) happening at its heart. A planet does not create its own light, and usually orbits a star.

A brown dwarf is bigger than a planet but it is not as big as a star. Because brown dwarfs are smaller than normal stars, they don't have the same temperatures and pressures in their cores to allow fusion to take place properly.

When a brown dwarf is born, it uses up its energy-generating fuel super quickly and then fizzles out. With its fuel gone, the brown dwarf cannot do any form of fusion, so it can't be considered a star. But now it is similar to a planet as it doesn't create its own light.

A BROWN DWARF

WHY ARE PLANETS ROUND?

Planets are round because of gravity, and the way gravity works. To make sense of this, let's start by looking at a bubble. If you have ever blown a bubble, you will notice that, after a few wobbles, it naturally becomes a round shape, or 'sphere'. This happens because when you blow the bubble you trap a small volume of air inside a thin film of soap.

All the molecules that make up the soapy film are attracted to each other, and they shrink together to form the smallest, tightest area possible – a sphere.

In a similar way, the force of gravity is strong enough to pull most planets into spheres. When planets form, gravity pulls the bits and pieces that make the planet in towards its centre. Think of it like the way the spokes on the wheel of your bike point inwards. As this force is equally balanced in every direction, the planet forms a sphere.

However, if an object is less than 20 km in diameter, the gravitational force is not strong enough to pull all of the material equally towards the middle. This is why smaller objects, such as asteroids, often have wonky shapes.

WHAT IS A BLACK HOLE?

A black hole is one of the strangest phenomena in space. It is an object that has a huge amount of mass – mass is the amount of 'stuff' in something. The more mass an object has, the greater its gravitational force. Black holes get their name because gravity is so *incredibly* strong around them that not even light can escape. Let's take a closer look ... without getting sucked in!

MINI TO MASSIVE

Black holes come in different sizes. Scientists think that mini black holes exist, which are tiny, but have a mass that's larger than a mountain's.

Larger ones, called stellar black holes, have a mass that's between three and ten times the mass of our Sun. While the Sun is 1.3 million km wide, a stellar black hole is squeezed into an area that can be just 30 km wide.

At the far end of the scale are super-massive black holes. These can have masses that are millions, possibly BILLIONS, of times greater than our Sun. One of these beasts sits at the centre of our Milky Way galaxy. There are others at the centres of other galaxies, too.

IT'S THOUGHT THERE ARE AROUND 10 MILLION TO 1 BILLION BLACK HOLES IN OUR MILKY WAY GALAXY.

STARS THAT STOP SHINING

Scientists aren't sure how super-massive black holes form, but stellar black holes are created at the end of a star's life, when the star runs out of fuel for fusion (pages 14–15).

During fusion, atoms get smushed together to form new elements and energy in the form of radiation. Albert Einstein's equation $E = mc^2$ describes this process. Radiation is what makes stars shine and it creates a powerful outward force. Meanwhile, the inward force of gravity holds the star together.

When the star runs out of fuel for fusion, the gravitational force becomes overwhelming and the star collapses in on itself. Sometimes, it leaves behind a dense core – also known as a black hole.

 ## HARD TO SPOT

As no light leaves a black hole, it can be hard to spot one. But even if we can't see a black hole, we can see the effect it has on other things. We can see stars orbiting and even swerving around black holes. If a star gets too close to a black hole, it gets sucked inside. As the star is torn apart by the black hole, it sends out streams of radiation that we can detect.

AN ILLUSTRATION OF A STAR BEING EATEN BY A BLACK HOLE

WHAT WOULD HAPPEN IF I FELL INTO A BLACK HOLE?

If you fell into a black hole it wouldn't be pleasant. You might expect to be crushed or blown up in a second, but the reality is even weirder ...

GETTING CLOSER

The pull of the black hole's gigantic gravitational force feels stronger the closer you get. The point of no return is called the 'event horizon'. This is an imaginary sphere that surrounds a black hole. Once you cross it, the force of gravity is so strong that you can't possibly escape. As you head towards the centre of the black hole, the laws of physics start to break down completely and things get pretty weird ... For instance, due to the immense gravity of the black hole, time slows down.

SPAGHETTIFIED

As you fall inside a black hole every part of you can feel the black hole's immense gravitational pull, but if you fall into the hole feet first then the force of gravity is stronger on your toes than on your head. This means that you get stretched out as if you are a really long noodle (painful!). An astronomer called Sir Martin Rees was the first to describe this process as 'spaghettification'.

AN ILLUSTRATION OF WHAT A BLACK HOLE MIGHT LOOK LIKE

Astro Fact

This all sounds scary, but there's no need to worry. Unless you go out of your way to visit a black hole, there's no chance you're going to fall into one. The nearest black hole to our Sun is about 1,500 light years away – too far to have any effect on us. Our Sun is also too small to turn into a black hole, so we are very safe on Earth.

WHAT ARE THE COLOURFUL CLOUDS IN SPACE MADE OF?

When we look into space with a powerful telescope, we can see all sorts of incredible things, including gigantic clouds. These clouds are called nebulae and they are made up of dust and gas (mainly hydrogen and helium) and the remains of old stars. When you look at nebulae with a telescope, they actually appear a grey colour. Their true beauty is only revealed when a long-exposure photo is taken with a telescope, and you get enough light to see their amazing colours.

LARGE BUT LIGHT

Nebulae are enormous. The largest known nebula is called the Tarantula nebula and it stretches for 1,800 light years across. In other words, it would take nearly 2,000 years for light to travel from one side of it to the other. Yikes!

However, although they are huge, nebulae have a very low density. This means that they don't have much mass for their size. For example, a nebula the size of our planet Earth would have a mass of just a few kilograms.

SOME NEBULAE FORM FROM THE MATTER THAT IS RELEASED INTO SPACE WHEN A MASSIVE STAR COLLAPSES.

NEAREST NEBULA

Using powerful telescopes, we can see nebulae of different shapes and sizes. Earth's nearest nebula is the Helix nebula, which sits 650 light years away.

The Helix nebula is an example of a planetary nebula. Planetary nebulae are nothing to do with planets – they are the remains of stars that would have looked a lot like our Sun. In 5 billion years, when our Sun dies, it will turn into a planetary nebula like the Helix.

THE HELIX NEBULA

OTHER NEBULAE MAKE UP REGIONS IN SPACE CALLED STELLAR NURSERIES. BABY STARS ARE BORN INSIDE THESE CLOUDS.

INTO THE CLOUDS

Launched into space in 2021, the James Webb Space Telescope may be able to give us a better understanding of nebulae. This special scope picks up infrared light from deep inside the clouds of dust, so we can see what lies at their cores.

ARE THERE OTHER PLANETS LIKE OURS?

In our Solar System, there are two planets that have some aspects that are similar to Earth – these are our closest neighbours, Venus and Mars. But if we look beyond our Solar System, it's possible we may one day find other planets very like Earth, orbiting different, distant stars.

VENUS

Venus is sometimes called Earth's twin because the two planets are similar in size, mass and structure. Both planets also have an atmosphere, but that is where the similarities end.

Venus has an atmosphere that is very thick – 100 times thicker than Earth's. Because of its thick atmosphere and its position close to the Sun, the temperature on Venus' surface is hot enough to melt lead.

MARS

Mars is also considered to be quite Earth-like in some ways. Although smaller than Earth, it has a similar structure – with an inner core, a mantle and a surface crust. Mars also has polar ice caps like Earth.

Mars has a thin atmosphere now, but evidence shows that, in the past, the red planet had a thicker atmosphere and water used to run over its surface.

EXOPLANETS

If we cast our search wider, beyond our Solar System, we find exoplanets – mysterious planets that orbit the stars that we see in the night sky. Some of these exoplanets are similar in size to Earth. In a few cases, we are able to analyse the atmospheres of these planets and we sometimes find planets with water vapour in their atmosphere, just like the water vapour in our own atmosphere.

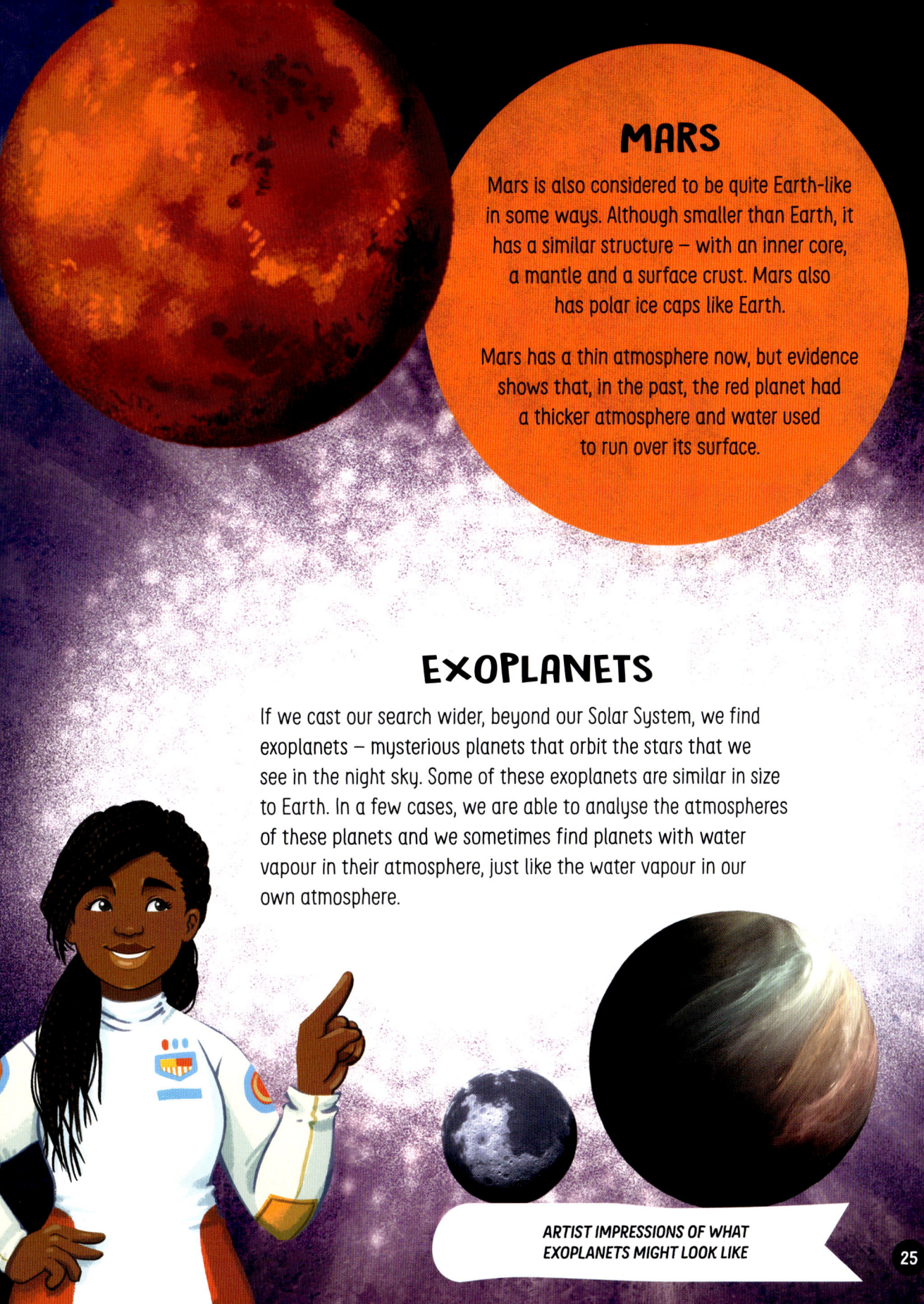

ARTIST IMPRESSIONS OF WHAT EXOPLANETS MIGHT LOOK LIKE

DOES LIFE EXIST ON OTHER PLANETS?

I think it might ... but we may have to search beyond the planets and moons of our Solar System. A spacecraft called Gaia has been looking at our Milky Way galaxy and revealed that it is home to around 300 billion stars. With improving technology, we are also discovering exoplanets (page 25) orbiting around these stars. To date, over 5,000 exoplanets have been found, and we're discovering more all the time.

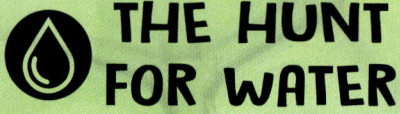

THE HUNT FOR WATER

One of the things that all life on Earth has in common is the need for liquid water. New technologies are allowing us to investigate the exoplanets beyond our Solar System and detect the chemicals that make up their atmospheres.

Excitingly, scientists have discovered water vapour in the atmospheres of some of these planets. This means there is potential for life that could have some similarities to our own on exoplanets billions of kilometres away from Earth.

IT ADDS UP

The reason I am pretty sure other forms of life are out there is because of the numbers. As technology gets better, we are finding more and more exoplanets. If every star in the Milky Way galaxy had just two planets orbiting it, that would mean there are at least 600 billion planets out there. Not all of them would be suitable for life – but it seems likely that some of them would.

Our galaxy is also thought to be one of 200 BILLION galaxies in the Universe. To my mind, with so many stars and planets out there, why would life just occur on Earth?

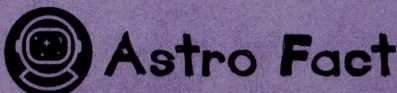

Astro Fact

If I met an alien, I'd try to look for something we'd have in common. An alien isn't going to understand English, but the laws of physics seem to be the same throughout the Universe – so an alien might be able to understand maths.

If we used maths as a starting point, we may then be able to find other ways to communicate with one another.

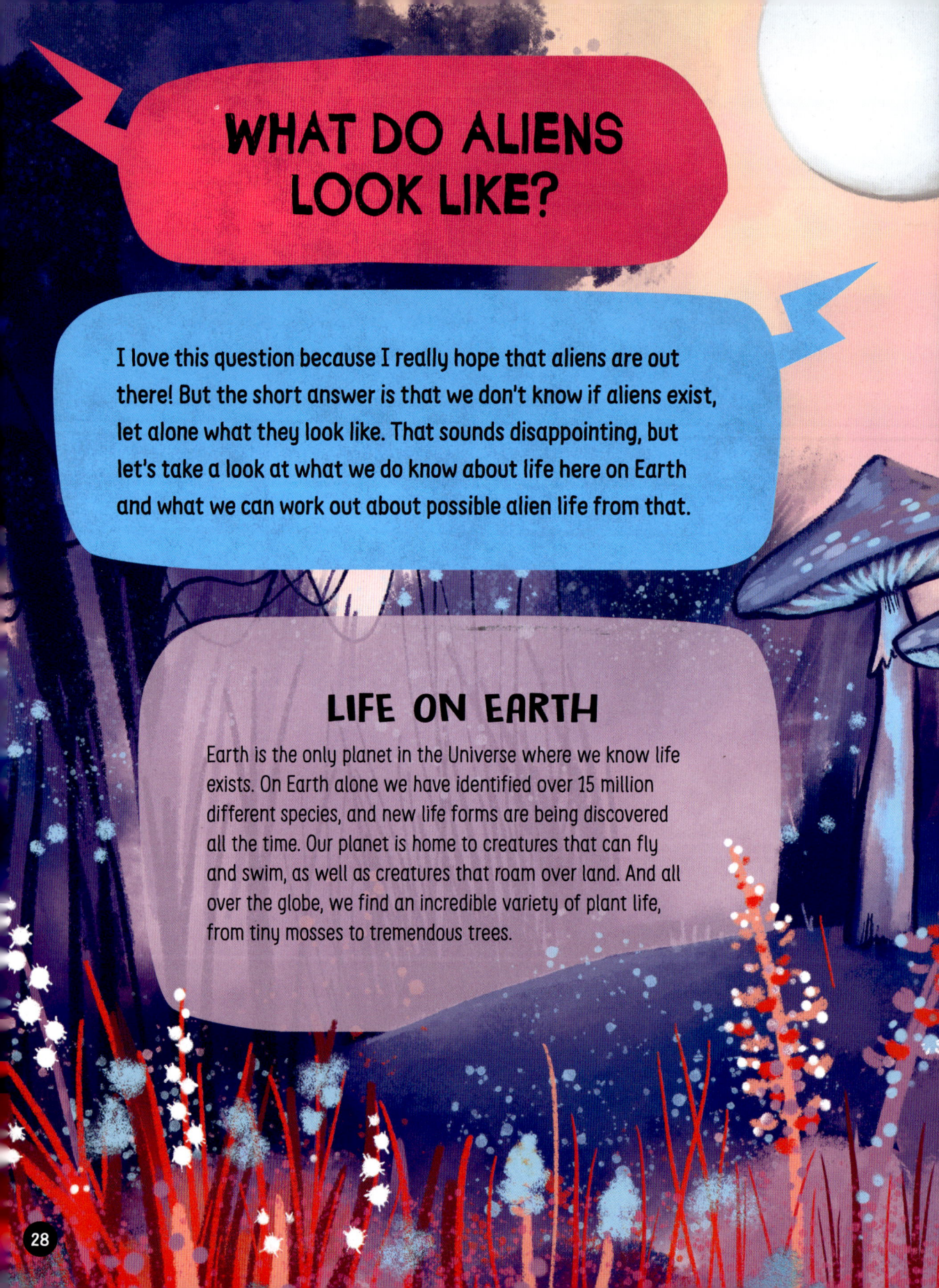

WHAT DO ALIENS LOOK LIKE?

I love this question because I really hope that aliens are out there! But the short answer is that we don't know if aliens exist, let alone what they look like. That sounds disappointing, but let's take a look at what we do know about life here on Earth and what we can work out about possible alien life from that.

LIFE ON EARTH

Earth is the only planet in the Universe where we know life exists. On Earth alone we have identified over 15 million different species, and new life forms are being discovered all the time. Our planet is home to creatures that can fly and swim, as well as creatures that roam over land. And all over the globe, we find an incredible variety of plant life, from tiny mosses to tremendous trees.

INCREDIBLE ADAPTATIONS

The main thing that seems to determine what a life form looks like is the environment that it lives in. For example, fish have gills so they can take in oxygen from the water to breathe, and giraffes have long necks so they can reach the tasty leaves at the top of acacia trees.

ALIEN WORLDS

So, although we don't know if aliens are out there, if aliens do exist we can probably tell something about their appearance by looking at the sort of planet they'd live on. As we look further and further out into space, we are discovering all sorts of different planets and moons with unique environments, from very cold planets to dry, dusty ones.

Because of the variety of planets and potential, undiscovered environments in the Universe, I think that most aliens would look very different from humans, unless they lived on a planet that was similar to Earth and orbited a star like our Sun.

WHAT IS THE 'MILKY WAY'?

Look up at the sky on a clear, cloudless night, away from street-lights and other light pollution, and you may see a dusty-looking path of stars. What you're looking at is part of our galaxy, the Milky Way. It is home to around 300 billion stars, 6,000 of which can be seen with the naked eye from Earth.

For thousands of years, people across the world have looked at this band of brightness and called it different names. To the !Kung people of the Kalahari Desert in Southern Africa, it is the 'Backbone of the Night', while in China it is known as the 'Silver River'. In many European cultures, it is called the 'Milky Way'. This name dates back to the ancient Greeks, who thought the stretch of stars looked like the milk of the gods. They named it 'via lactea', which is where our 'Milky Way' comes from.

ARE THERE OTHER GALAXIES?

Absolutely! In fact, astronomers think there could be up to 200 billion galaxies out there. This wasn't always the case, though. A hundred years ago, astronomers believed that our galaxy was the only one in the Universe. Other fuzzy spirals of light had been spotted through telescopes since the 17th century, but they were thought to be part of the Milky Way.

In 1924, an astronomer called Edwin Hubble took a closer look at one of these fuzzy spirals. He realized that there were individual stars inside it, including a special type of star that pulsed light (pages 8–9). These stars had already been studied by an astronomer called Henrietta Leavitt. She had created an equation that allowed scientists to work out how far away these stars were based on how often they pulsed.

Hubble used Leavitt's equation to work out that the stars in the spiral were 2.5 million light years away, far more distant than the stars in our Milky Way. He realized that he was looking at a separate galaxy – the Andromeda galaxy – and that all the fuzzy spirals of light he could see were other, distant galaxies.

THE ANDROMEDA GALAXY

HOW WILL THE UNIVERSE END?

We don't know how the Universe will end, but we do know that it won't be for many, many billions of years. We know that the Universe has been expanding since the time of the Big Bang (pages 8–9). What happens to the Universe in the future depends on whether this expansion carries on, stops or goes into reverse. These are the three main theories that describe what could happen.

1. CRUNCH TIME

A theory called the 'Big Crunch' considers what would happen if the Universe stopped expanding and started to shrink. This could happen because the combined gravity of all the mass and dark matter in the Universe would be large enough to slow the rate of expansion. Dark matter is the stuff that we cannot see, but we know exists because we can measure the effect of its gravity on other things. This could mean that at some point in the very, very distant future, matter in the Universe would start to lump together, which would be the opposite of what happened during the Big Bang.

UNTIL THE 20TH CENTURY, PEOPLE THOUGHT THAT THE UNIVERSE WAS UNCHANGING. THE WORK OF ASTRONOMERS SUCH AS EDWIN HUBBLE (PAGE 8) CHALLENGED THIS IDEA.

NASA ARE CURRENTLY WORKING ON A NEW SPACE TELESCOPE THAT WILL ALLOW SCIENTISTS TO STUDY DARK ENERGY.

2. BBB-RRRR!

The problem with the 'Big Crunch' theory is that the rate at which the Universe expands seems to have sped up over time, not slowed down. Scientists aren't sure why this happens, but they think this speeding up is caused by a mysterious force known as dark energy.

If the Universe keeps on expanding, then in billions of years' time, we might get what scientists call the 'Big Freeze'. In the Big Freeze theory, everything would get colder and colder, stars and galaxies would no longer form and the Universe would become a dark place.

3. THE BIG RIP

The final scenario for the Universe is called the 'Big Rip'. This is where dark energy dominates and overcomes the other gravitational forces. In this theory, the expansion would happen so quickly that galaxies, solar systems and eventually atoms would be ripped apart. But don't worry – whatever the future holds for the Universe, none of this will happen for billions or even TRILLIONS of years.

CHAPTER 2: OUR SOLAR SYSTEM

Things start to feel more familiar in this chapter as we take a look at our nearest neighbours – the Sun (our local star), the eight planets that orbit it, and the dwarf planets, moons, asteroids and other objects that make up our Solar System. Beyond our Solar System, there are countless other groups of planets orbiting their own stars. But our system is special – so far, it is the only one we know that supports life.

HOW BIG IS THE SUN?

The simple answer is very, very, VERY big. The Sun contains 99.8% of all of the mass in our Solar System. All the other planets, dwarf planets, moons, comets and asteroids make up the remaining 0.2%.

THE SUN

SIZE OF EARTH

BIG ...

This gets more mind-boggling when we compare the size of the Sun to the size of Earth. You'd be able to fit one million planet Earths into our Sun — 1.3 million if you squished them up really tight and left no gaps. Another way of thinking of it is to imagine that the Sun is a basketball. Earth would be smaller than one of the tiny bumps on the ball's surface.

... AND BIGGER

When it's compared to Earth, the Sun seems huge. But when the Sun is compared to other stars it is about average. Many stars are much bigger – and some are over 100 times bigger!

Let's take a look at an example of a really enormous star to get a sense of this. Betelgeuse is a star that can be seen in the constellation of Orion. It is a type of star called a 'red supergiant' and it certainly lives up to its name. Some scientists estimate that we could fit around one million Suns inside Betelgeuse.

THE ORION CONSTELLATION – THE ORANGE STAR IN THE TOP LEFT IS BETELGEUSE.

SIZE OF THE SUN

BETELGEUSE

HOW CLOSE COULD A SPACESHIP GET TO THE SUN BEFORE IT MELTED?

A giant ball of gas large enough to contain over a million Earths and with an atmospheric temperature of over 1 million °C, the Sun is an incredibly hot place. We know to never look directly at the Sun ... so flying straight at it surely isn't a good idea, right? Well, currently, one robotic mission is doing just that.

TO BOLDLY GO ...

Parker, a NASA space probe, is getting closer to the surface of the Sun than any other spacecraft has before. In 2021, it became the first spacecraft to fly through the Sun's outer atmosphere, called the corona, and it is aiming to get within 7 million km of the Sun's surface by 2025. At its closest, Parker will heat up to around 1400 °C. That's about five times hotter than the top temperature on your kitchen oven!

THE PARKER SPACE PROBE GETS ITS NAME FROM A PIONEERING PHYSICIST CALLED EUGENE PARKER. IT'S THE FIRST NASA SPACECRAFT TO BE NAMED AFTER A LIVING PERSON.

LINES OF DEFENCE

To stop Parker from melting like cheese, it is kitted out with several ingenious technologies. It has a heat shield made up of a carbon foam sandwiched between two carbon slices. Carbon is a great conductor, meaning it transfers heat. This stops the probe from getting too warm. The outside of the shield is coated in a special white paint, which reflects heat back to the Sun.

Parker also has a water-cooling system that cools down critical areas. In addition to this, the probe can control its own movements. If it senses that things are getting too hot, it will move into a cooler position so it doesn't overheat.

☼ CLOSER STILL

With all these accessories, Parker will be able to get amazingly close to the Sun. In doing so, it will collect data that can give us a better understanding of the Sun and how it affects us on Earth. For now, 7 million km is as near as a spacecraft can comfortably get but, in the future, more hi-tech materials might allow us to get even closer to the Sun.

WHY ISN'T MERCURY THE HOTTEST PLANET?

Mercury is the planet closest to the Sun and, as you'd expect, it's a pretty toasty place. Surface temperatures on Mercury can reach around 430 °C. That's super-hot compared to Earth's average of 15 °C. But Mercury is not the hottest planet in the Solar System. That title goes to Venus, where temperatures can reach a scorching 471 °C. This is all to do with the thickness of the planets' atmospheres and what gases they contain.

CHANGE IN TEMPERATURE

Although temperatures on the 'day side' of Mercury — the side of the planet facing the Sun — can reach 430 °C, it's a different story on the night side. There, the temperature plummets to a chilly −180 °C. That's twice as cold as the coldest temperature ever recorded in Antarctica! These huge contrasts are due to the fact that Mercury has a very thin atmosphere. This means that any heating up that takes place on the day side isn't transferred to the night side. Mercury also rotates on its axis very slowly, so only certain parts of the surface get a chance to heat up at a time.

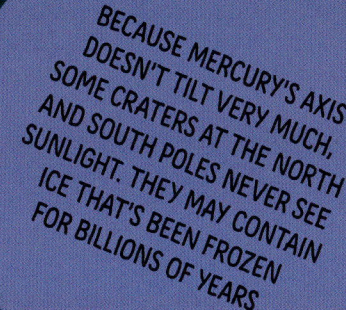

BECAUSE MERCURY'S AXIS DOESN'T TILT VERY MUCH, SOME CRATERS AT THE NORTH AND SOUTH POLES NEVER SEE SUNLIGHT. THEY MAY CONTAIN ICE THAT'S BEEN FROZEN FOR BILLIONS OF YEARS.

 GETTING HOT

In contrast, Venus has an extremely thick atmosphere that is mainly made up of carbon dioxide (CO_2). CO_2 is also found in the atmosphere on Earth where it is known as a greenhouse gas. This is because CO_2 absorbs heat, trapping it within Earth's atmosphere and making our planet warmer.

On Earth, CO_2 makes up 0.04% of the atmosphere, but on Venus it accounts for a staggering 96%. It's thanks to all this CO_2 that Venus is hotter than Mercury. With so much CO_2 packed into its atmosphere, Venus is undergoing a very extreme form of global warming, making the planet hotter than all the others.

VENUS' ATMOSPHERE IS 90 TIMES MORE DENSE THAN EARTH'S.

CAN I SEE ANY PLANETS IN THE NIGHT SKY FROM EARTH?

You can! In fact, you can see Mercury, Venus, Mars, Jupiter and Saturn using just your eyes. Because Uranus and Neptune are a long way away from Earth, you normally need binoculars or a telescope to see them – though it's just about possible to glimpse Uranus with the naked eye at the right time of year.

KEEP AN EYE OUT

Different planets can be seen at different times throughout the year. This is because of the way they move around the Sun. Like Earth, the planets move in an orbit around the Sun, but each planet takes a different amount of time to finish one orbit. Earth takes one year, or 365 and a quarter days, to orbit the Sun. Planets that are closer to the Sun complete their orbits more quickly. Mercury, for example, takes 88 days. Planets that are further away take longer. Saturn takes 29 Earth years to finish one orbit!

Because the planets are moving around the Sun at different speeds, they appear in Earth's night sky at different times. Planets can be seen most clearly when they are in 'opposition'. This is when the Earth sits between the Sun and another planet. In this position, we can see the planet fully lit up by the Sun. The planet is on the 'opposite' side of Earth compared to the Sun.

JUPITER

Despite being the largest planet in the Solar System, Jupiter isn't usually as bright as Venus because it is much further away from Earth. If you look at Jupiter with a telescope, you should be able to spot some of its moons.

VENUS

After the Moon, Venus is the brightest thing in the night sky and it can be seen before sunrise or after sunset. Because of this, it's sometimes called the Morning Star or the Evening Star (even though it's a planet, not a star).

MARS

Mars is an easy planet to identify because it has an orange-red colour when seen in the sky.

SATURN

Saturn looks like a bright, golden star in the night sky. You'll need a telescope to see its rings.

MERCURY

Because its orbit is very close to the Sun, we can only see Mercury soon after sunset or just before sunrise. It is normally very low on the horizon.

 Try This At Home

Pick a clear, cloud-free night and go planet spotting. A simple way to tell if you are looking at a star or a planet is to see how much it twinkles – planets don't twinkle as much as stars. There are some good apps that can help, too!

QUICK QUESTIONS ON ...
MOONS

WHY DO SOME PLANETS HAVE MORE MOONS THAN OTHERS?

Planets close to the Sun don't have as many moons as planets that are further away. Most of the dust and gas that wasn't used when the planet formed was sucked up by the Sun, rather than clumping up to make moons. The outer planets are also more massive, so they have stronger gravitational fields and can pull more moons towards them.

WHICH PLANET HAS THE LARGEST MOON?

Jupiter's Ganymede is the largest moon in the Solar System. It is actually larger than the planet Mercury and generates its own magnetic field. It's so big that if it was orbiting the Sun rather than Jupiter, it would be considered a planet.

GANYMEDE

HOW DOES THE MOON AFFECT LIFE ON EARTH?

The Moon acts like an anchor to Earth. The gentle tug of the Moon's gravity slows down the speed of Earth's spin, influencing the length of our days and creating tides in our oceans. It also helps to steady Earth on its axis. Without the Moon, the Earth would wobble about on its axis and this would make our planet's climate very unstable. Some people also believe that the Moon's effect on the tides helped to create early life on Earth.

WHY DO PEOPLE SAY THE MOON IS MADE OF CHEESE?

This myth has been around for hundreds of years. It's based on the way the craters on the Moon's surface look like holes in a cheese. One of the earliest known stories is a folk tale about a fox being chased by a wolf. To distract the wolf, the fox tells him that a reflection of the Moon in a lake is actually a giant cheese. The wolf drinks the water so he can gobble up the cheese ... and the fox escapes!

IS THERE NIGHT AND DAY ON THE MOON?

There is – but a whole day on the Moon is quite different to a whole day on Earth.

NIGHT AND DAY

Here on Earth we experience night and day because the planet spins on its axis. The axis is an imaginary line through the middle of the planet, running from the North to the South Pole. It takes 24 hours for the Earth to complete one spin on its axis. As it spins, the half of the planet pointing towards the Sun has its day. The half that is not pointing towards the Sun has its night.

A similar thing happens on the Moon, but the Moon's rotation on its axis is MUCH slower than Earth's. It takes the Moon about 27 Earth days to rotate just once on its axis. Talk about a long day!

 HOT AND COLD

The day-time and night-time temperatures on the Moon feel very extreme compared to those on Earth. Day-time temperatures on the Moon reach a whopping 120 °C and drop to a frosty −130 °C during the night. This is because the Moon has virtually no atmosphere, so there is nothing to absorb the Sun's rays on the day side or transfer the heat to the night side.

EARTH TILTS ON ITS AXIS BY ABOUT 23 DEGREES. IT IS THIS TILT THAT GIVES US OUR SEASONS. THE MOON HAS A VERY SMALL TILT IN COMPARISON – ABOUT 1.5 DEGREES. THIS MEANS THERE ARE SOME PLACES ON THE MOON THAT NEVER GET SUNLIGHT.

WHY DON'T PEOPLE WALK UPSIDE DOWN ON THE BOTTOM OF EARTH?

The simple answer is 'gravity', but this question raises lots of interesting ideas about how we view our place in the world. And that has a lot to do with maps.

THE HISTORY BIT

Maps haven't always had north at the 'top'. Many ancient Egyptian maps put east, the direction of sunrise, at the top. Early Islamic map-makers put south at the top because Mecca, the most important city in the religion of Islam, lay south of their land.

In the 1600s, European sailors started exploring the world and drew up maps to chart their discoveries. Because the explorers came from the northern part of the world and used the North star to find their way home, they put north at the top. This became the standard map style.

From space, we can see that the Earth doesn't have a 'top' or 'bottom'. But that doesn't stop people putting a 'north-up' view on the world.

A famous photo called the Blue Marble (left) was taken by NASA in 1972. As you can see, Antarctica is at the top of the photo. But later on, NASA flipped the photo to put Antarctica at the bottom, so people wouldn't get muddled.

'THE BLUE MARBLE'

THE SCIENCE BIT

So, maps make us think there is a 'top' and 'bottom' to Earth when there's no such thing. The reason we can all walk about anywhere on the surface of Earth the right way up (and without floating off into space) is down to our old friend, gravity.

We see gravity at work all around us. If you knock a glass off a table, it will fall to the floor. Or if you jump up in the air, you'll come back to land on the ground. This is because Earth's gravity acts as if it is pulling everything in towards the planet's centre. Wherever you are on the planet, the Earth's centre is what gravity considers to be 'down', and the opposite direction is 'up'.

HAS THERE EVER BEEN LIFE ON MARS?

Mars is one of the planets that you can see in Earth's night sky using just your eyes. People have been looking up at Mars and wondering if any life exists on it for thousands of years. To date, none of the missions we've sent to Mars have found evidence of life, past or present. But this may change as technology gets better.

EARLY EVIDENCE

During the 1800s, the invention of large telescopes allowed people to see Mars more clearly. Some astronomers thought they could spot canals on the planet and decided there must be life there. This caused excitement, but as technology got better these 'canals' were shown to be optical illusions caused by craters on the planet's surface.

In 1964–65, we were able to send a spacecraft to Mars for the first time. Since then, many missions have flown by or landed on the red planet, but no evidence of life has been found yet. The main problem is that Mars' atmosphere is very thin – it's too thin for us humans to breathe – and radiation from the Sun is likely to kill living creatures on the surface.

 A WATERY WORLD

We think things *might* have lived on Mars in the past because evidence of water has been found on the planet. Studies of its structure have shown that between 3 and 4 billion years ago, water flowed all over Mars. In fact, there was so much water that Mars would once have been covered in pools, lakes and even oceans. Here on Earth, where there is water, there is a possibility of life.

MISSION TO MARS

The problem with missions to Mars up till now is that they have relied entirely on experiments conducted by rovers on the planet. It hasn't been possible to send back any of the evidence gathered by these rovers to Earth. In 2021, a new rover called Perseverance landed on Mars. Perseverance's mission is to look for signs of life and collect samples that can be sent back to Earth. The samples will be studied by scientists using sophisticated equipment on Earth for the first time. This means that we may finally be able to answer the question of whether there is, or was, life on Mars.

NASA'S PERSEVERANCE ROVER

HOW DO YOU LAND A SPACESHIP ON MARS?

Called 'the seven minutes of terror' by scientists, landing a spacecraft on Mars is a nail-biting process. Two main challenges have to be overcome: the pull of the planet's gravity making the spacecraft fall too fast, and the heat generated as the craft travels through the atmosphere. To see what's involved, let's take a look at how one rover, Perseverance, did it in 2021.

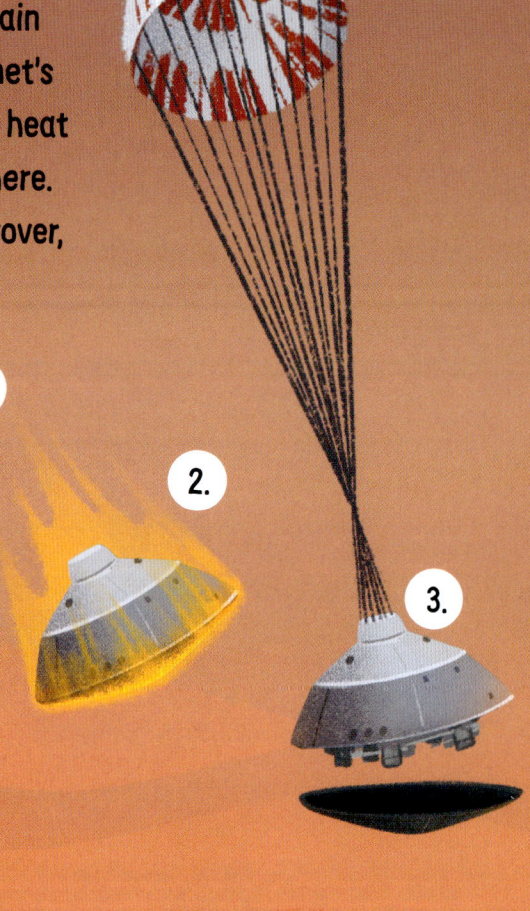

1.

Just before it reached Mars' atmosphere, Perseverance got rid of the parts it had needed during its flight to the planet. Only the rover and the landing equipment were left. The craft was travelling at about 20,000 km per hour.

2.

When it entered the atmosphere, the craft slowed down due to air resistance. It was also exposed to temperatures of 1,300 °C due to atmospheric heating. Perseverance's protective shell and heat shield kept it safe and cool.

3.

Once the craft slowed down to under 1,600 km per hour, a giant parachute opened. This slowed the craft further. The temperatures were now safe, so the heat shield was let loose.

4.

Mars has a thin atmosphere, so a parachute can only slow a craft down to about 320 km per hour. The parachute was jettisoned and another device, called a retrorocket, was used to bring Perseverance to a standstill.

5.

The retrorocket was made up of eight engines pointing at the ground, which slowed the craft down. The force of the rockets worked against the pull of Mars' gravity on the spacecraft. This meant Perseverance headed towards the surface at a gentle speed.

6.

The final stage involved a skycrane. This was a cable that lowered the rover down to the surface. When the rover's wheels hit the ground, the skycrane was cut loose and flew away from the rover. Perseverance had touched down!

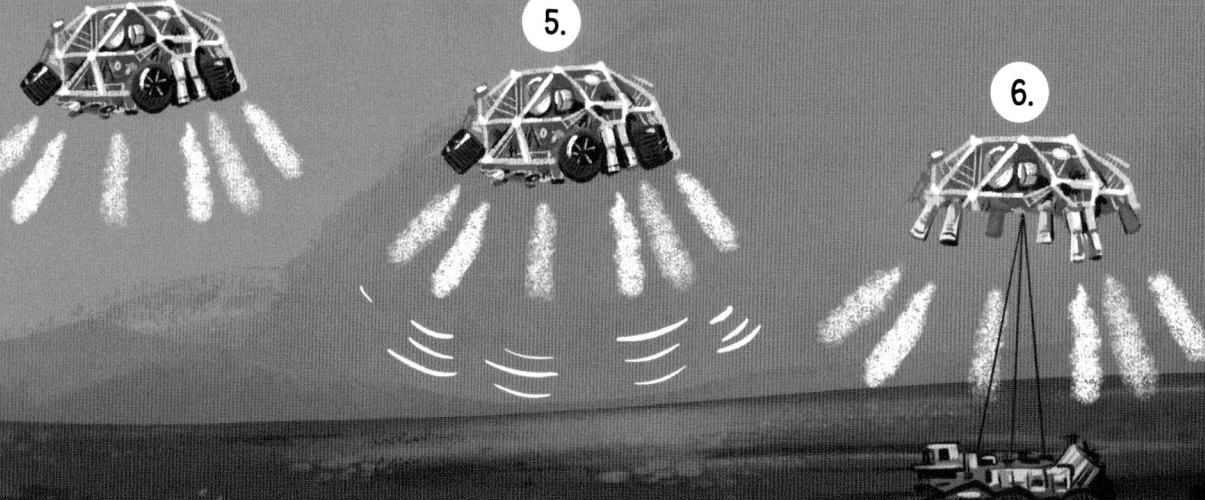

HOW MANY ROVERS HAVE BEEN TO MARS?

A rover is a vehicle made to explore the surface of a planet or moon. These busy machines collect data that is sent back to scientists on Earth. Sending a rover anywhere is a risky business but, to date, there have been six successful rover missions to Mars.

1: SOJOURNER

The first successful Mars rover was NASA's Sojourner, which landed in July 1997. Named after Sojourner Truth, an African-American human-rights activist, it operated for 85 days, took over 550 photos, and studied Mars' rocks and weather. Sojourner was only the size of a microwave oven, but it represented a gigantic step in the study of Mars.

SOJOURNER ON MARS

2 & 3: SPIRIT & OPPORTUNITY

Twin rovers called Spirit and Opportunity were sent to opposite sides of the planet in 2004. Spirit spent over six years roaming around and Opportunity lasted for 14 years. Both showed that Mars used to have liquid water on its surface.

A PHOTO OF THE MARTIAN SURFACE TAKEN BY OPPORTUNITY.

CURIOSITY HAS TAKEN LOTS OF SELFIES!

4: CURIOSITY

Curiosity landed in 2012 and is still trundling around Mars today. The size of a small car, Curiosity is equipped with instruments so it can analyse the planet's surface.

5: ZHURONG

China has already sent two rovers to the Moon, but Zhurong is the country's first rover to reach another planet. It touched down in 2021 and its mission is to study Mars' atmosphere, soil and landscape.

THE AREA OF MARS THAT ZHURONG IS EXPLORING.

INGENUITY ON MARS

6: PERSEVERANCE

Perseverance touched down in 2021, and brought a sidekick with it – a mini helicopter called Ingenuity. Ingenuity was the first machine to fly on another planet. It is helping Perseverance to navigate Mars' rocky terrain, as the rover searches for signs of ancient life.

COULD I LAND ON A COMET?

Comets are made from dust, rock and ice that was left behind when the Solar System formed. They often travel way out beyond the orbit of Neptune, before being drawn back into the inner Solar System by the Sun's gravity. Taking a ride on a comet would be amazing fun. But landing on one would be a challenge ...

TOUCH DOWN

Over the years, we have flown past comets, collected the particles left behind by comets, and even deliberately crashed into them. To date, we have had just one successful landing on a comet. This was made by a robotic probe called Philae, which touched down on a comet called 67P/Churyumov-Gerasimenko on 12th November, 2014. So, could a person do the same?

LIFE ON A COMET

Because comets are small, their gravitational force is very weak. This means that staying put on a comet's surface is tricky. The Philae probe had harpoons that would fire once it reached the comet's surface to secure it. If you wanted to land on a comet, you would need to take similar precautions to avoid floating off into space. You'd also need a spacesuit to protect you from the Sun's radiation and the bitterly cold temperatures in the outer Solar System. The suit would have to provide you with air to breathe and water and food to survive, too.

WHEN PHILAE LANDED, ITS HARPOONS DIDN'T WORK AND THE POOR PROBE BOUNCED ACROSS THE COMET BEFORE ENDING UP IN A CREVICE. OUT OF DIRECT SUNLIGHT, IT WAS UNABLE TO CHARGE ITS SOLAR-POWERED BATTERIES AND EVENTUALLY RAN OUT OF POWER.

Astro Fact

If you landed on a comet, you'd need to keep an eye on its orbit. As a comet approaches the Sun, it heats up, and dust and gas leave the comet, forming a tail. During this stage, things get a little unstable, so this would be a good time to head home!

DOES IT REALLY RAIN DIAMONDS ON JUPITER?

No person has ever explored the depths of Jupiter's atmosphere – all our observations have been made from a distance. This means it's hard to know for certain what's going on there. Diamonds falling from the sky sounds like the stuff of science-fiction movies, but scientists are pretty sure that gemstones the size of your thumb could be raining down inside the giant planet.

DIAMOND GEOLOGY

To understand how this could happen, let's look at how diamonds are formed on Earth.

Most natural diamonds were formed billions of years ago in the planet's 'mantle' – the layer of rock that lies between the Earth's crust and its core. The mantle contains a mineral called graphite, which is a form of the element carbon.

Temperatures in the mantle are incredibly hot and pressures are very high. Under these conditions, the carbon atoms in the graphite got squeezed together. Eventually, this combination of heat, pressure and squeezing transformed the carbon into diamond. These transformations took place hundreds of kilometres below the Earth's crust, but volcanic activity over time pushed the diamonds up to the surface.

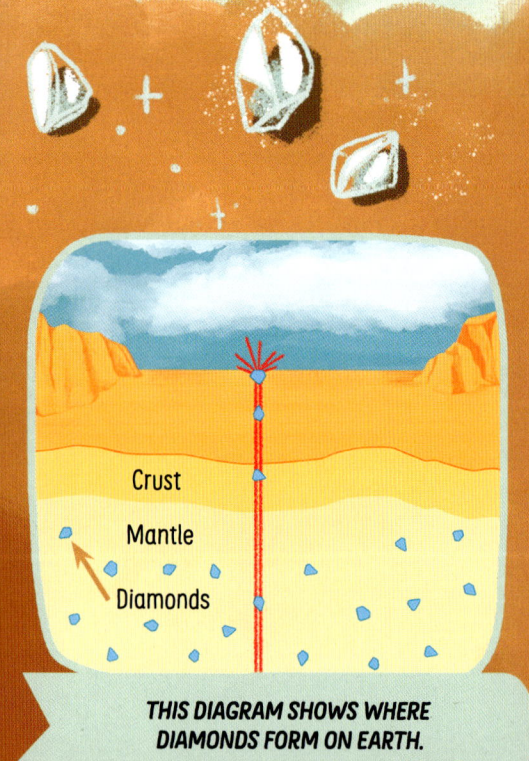

THIS DIAGRAM SHOWS WHERE DIAMONDS FORM ON EARTH.

💧 IT'S RAINING GEMS!

If diamonds on Earth are formed underground, how do they fall from the sky on Jupiter? It comes down to the special conditions found in the planet's atmosphere.

Jupiter has a dense atmosphere that's rich in methane. Methane is a molecule that's made up of the elements carbon and hydrogen. The planet also experiences storms and lightning regularly arcs through its clouds.

When methane in the atmosphere is struck by lightning, the molecules split into hydrogen and a type of carbon called soot. This soot is then believed to fall as rain. Like the conditions in Earth's mantle, the temperatures and pressures in Jupiter's atmosphere are extremely high. High enough to change the falling soot into a sparkling shower of diamonds.

DIAMOND RAIN IS THOUGHT TO FALL ON SATURN, TOO. SCIENTISTS THINK THE RINGED PLANET MAY PRODUCE 1,000 TONNES OF DIAMONDS A YEAR!

WHAT IS JUPITER'S 'GREAT RED SPOT'?

One of the Solar System's most spectacular sights, Jupiter's 'Great Red Spot' is an ever-swirling storm that sits in the planet's atmosphere. It is HUGE, around 1.3 times the size of Earth, and is the largest storm in the Solar System.

SCIENTISTS AREN'T SURE WHAT GIVES THE SPOT ITS RED COLOUR, BUT IT MAY BE TO DO WITH CHEMICALS BEING DRAWN UP FROM LOWER DOWN IN THE ATMOSPHERE.

EYE OF THE STORM

The storm is like a giant version of a hurricane, and stretches 300 km down into Jupiter's atmosphere. It swirls around in an anticlockwise direction at incredibly high speeds. The outer clouds of the storm spin faster than the inner clouds, and can reach speeds of over 640 km per hour – that's more than twice the speed of the fastest hurricane ever recorded on Earth.

A CLOSE-UP OF THE GREAT RED SPOT

SPOTTED!

The storm has been spinning for at least the last few centuries. Records of 'spots' on Jupiter date back to 1665, but the first official sighting was made by an astronomer called Samuel Heinrich Schwabe in 1831. Schwabe drew what he described as a 'hollow' on Jupiter's surface. In 1878, the storm was recorded by another astronomer, Carr Waller Pritchett, and it has been carefully watched by professional and amateur planet-gazers around the world ever since.

ALTHOUGH YOU NEED A STRONG TELESCOPE TO VIEW THE SPOT IN DETAIL, IT CAN BE SEEN WITH NON-PROFESSIONAL EQUIPMENT FROM EARTH.

 Astro Fact

Astronomers have noticed that the spot is getting smaller and more circular. In 1879, it measured 40,000 km across, but nowadays it is about 15,000 km. Some astronomers have even suggested that the spot could disappear in the next 20 years.

COULD I SLIDE AROUND SATURN'S RINGS?

From far away, Saturn's rings look like the perfect cosmic ice rink, but it would be impossible to land – let alone slide – around them. Let's get up close to see why.

SATURN'S RINGS ORBIT THE PLANET AND THEY ALL MOVE AT DIFFERENT SPEEDS. THE OUTER RINGS ARE SLOWER THAN THE HIGH-SPEED INNER RINGS.

RING AROUND

Saturn is circled by seven main rings, which are each made up of hundreds of smaller rings, or 'ringlets'. Scientists think there could be as many as 1,000 ringlets around the planet. The rings span an incredible distance, stretching up to 280,000 km across. That's as wide as 22 planet Earths! Although the rings cover a huge area, they're thin in comparison – they can be as little as 10 metres thick.

INSIDE THE RINGS

From far off, the rings look solid, but if you were to get up close, you'd see they are actually made of billions of separate, floating lumps of ice and rock. These lumps are all sorts of sizes – they can be as small as grains of sand to as big as mountains. Because the rings aren't one continuous, smooth circle of matter, it would be really hard to slide or even stand on them. It would be wiser to fly through them in a spaceship – just watch out for the bigger lumps!

ANCIENT RINGS

Some scientists think the lumps are bits of asteroids, comets or moons that were pulled in by Saturn's super-strong gravity and broken up due to collisions over the years. Others think that the rings are made from debris that was left behind when the planet first formed. This means that the rings could be as young as 100 million years or as old as the Solar System itself (4.5 billion years).

THE RINGS WERE FIRST SEEN THROUGH A TELESCOPE BY THE ASTRONOMER GALILEO GALILEI IN 1610. MORE RECENTLY, THEY WERE OBSERVED IN CLOSE-UP BY THE CASSINI-HUYGENS SPACE PROBE, WHICH ORBITED SATURN BETWEEN 2004 AND 2017.

WHY IS URANUS ON ITS SIDE?

The Solar System can seem a calm place, with planets moving around the Sun in orderly orbits. But billions of years ago, things were more unpredictable, and the planets were pummelled by giant lumps of rock and ice. A collision with an Earth-sized rock is what's thought to have knocked Uranus off-centre, and made it the only planet in the Solar System that spins on its side.

TREMENDOUS TILT

Uranus tilts on its axis at an angle of over 90 degrees. This is colossal when you compare it to the tilts of other planets in the Solar System. Venus, for instance, has a tilt of 2.6 degrees, while Earth has a tilt of just over 23 degrees.

Because Uranus spins around the Sun at such an extreme angle, sometimes the north of the planet is closest to the Sun, sometimes the south, and sometimes the equator. This leads to some pretty wild seasons during the course of one year – which, on Uranus, lasts for around 84 Earth years!

WOBBLY WORLD

Just like Earth and many of the other planets, Uranus has a magnetic field that is generated in its core and extends out beyond its surface. But Uranus' magnetic field is very lopsided. The axis of Earth's magnetic field is only 11 degrees off from the planet's axis of rotation. On Uranus, this angle is a mighty 60 degrees off.

ODD AURORAS

The impact of Uranus' wobbly magnetic field can be seen in the planet's auroras — the dancing displays of light that we call the Northern or Southern Lights on Earth. Auroras occur when charged particles from the Sun collide with a planet's magnetic field, and tend to be strongest at the North and South poles. Because of Uranus' tilt and wonky magnetic field, the planet's auroras aren't in line with the poles and they are more short-lived than those on Earth.

THE FUZZY WHITE PATCH IS AN AURORA ON URANUS.

WHAT MAKES NEPTUNE BLUE?

Neptune gets its blue colour because of chemicals in its atmosphere. We were able to take a closer look at the make-up of Neptune's atmosphere thanks to a spacecraft called Voyager 2, the only human-made object to fly past the planet to date. On 25th August, 1989, Voyager 2 travelled about 5,000 km above Neptune's north pole and took photos that revealed the planet's stunning blue shade.

SOMETHING IN THE AIR

Voyager 2 (see right) had various pieces of equipment on board to collect information about the planets it encountered. One was an instrument called a 'spectrometer', which allowed the spacecraft to analyse the planet's atmosphere.

We can see the planets in our Solar System because they reflect the Sun's light. A spectrometer can take that reflected light and analyse it. Different elements in an atmosphere absorb different colours of light. By analysing the light that is reflected from a planet, it is possible to work out what chemicals make up its atmosphere.

NEPTUNE WAS THE FIRST PLANET TO BE DISCOVERED USING MATHS. BY CALCULATING THE MOVEMENT OF SATURN, MATHEMATICIANS WERE ABLE TO WORK OUT THAT THERE WAS ANOTHER PLANET IN THE OUTER SOLAR SYSTEM.

ELECTRIC BLUE

Voyager 2 revealed that Neptune's atmosphere was made up of hydrogen, helium and methane. Methane is a simple chemical made up of hydrogen and carbon and it absorbs red light. This means that when sunlight reaches Neptune's atmosphere, the red light is absorbed, leaving just the blue light to be reflected. This is how Neptune gets its incredible, bright-blue colour.

IS PLUTO A PLANET?

Sitting far out in the icy regions beyond Neptune lies Pluto. When I was growing up, Pluto was considered the ninth planet in the Solar System but it is now classed as a dwarf planet.

This change happened in 2006. Pluto is a tiny world — smaller than our Moon — and other small bodies had been discovered that were a similar size or bigger than it, so the International Astronomical Union decided that they needed to create a definition of what made an astronomical body.

The new rules stated that a planet needs to:

1) orbit a star
2) have enough mass to be roughly spherical
3) have enough mass to dominate its orbit. In other words, it needed to be gravitationally big enough to clear its orbit of other cosmic bodies.

Pluto doesn't meet this final requirement, so it was reclassified as a dwarf planet. Although little Pluto is no longer considered a planet, it is a fascinating place, with hazy blue skies, red snow and a heart-shaped icy plain.

PLUTO

ARE THERE OTHER DWARF PLANETS?

At the moment, there are five official dwarf planets within our Solar System. As well as Pluto, the four official dwarf planets that we know of are called Ceres, Makemake, Haumea and Eris.

Ceres is the closest-known dwarf planet to Earth. It is located in the Asteroid Belt, between Mars and Jupiter.

The other dwarf planets are found, like Pluto, in a region of icy objects called the Kuiper Belt, which sits beyond Neptune. Haumea is perhaps the weirdest of the bunch. This titchy world is about the same size as Pluto but it spins super fast on its axis – it does one spin every four hours. The speed of its spins has turned the dwarf planet from a sphere into an 'ovoid' (a squished sphere).

CERES

HAUMEA

As technology gets better, we're finding more and more dwarf planets out there. Some of the recent finds include Orcus, Sedna, Quaoar and Gonggong. These worlds have been detected but are awaiting confirmation of their status as official dwarf planets.

QUICK QUESTIONS ON...
SHOOTING STARS

WHAT IS A SHOOTING STAR?

Despite what its name suggests, a shooting star is not a star but a small piece of dust or rock. Because it is travelling so fast, when it hits Earth's atmosphere it heats up due to friction and burns bright. As a shooting star burns, it leaves a trail of light across the sky. The colour of the trail depends on what kind of chemicals are burning in the debris, so we can work out what a shooting star is made of by studying its trail. Shooting stars are also called meteors.

WHEN CAN I SEE THEM?

The fantastic thing about shooting stars is that you don't need special equipment to see them – you can just use your eyes! The best time to see lots of shooting stars is during a meteor shower. These occur when Earth passes through a debris trail left behind by a comet. As the bits of debris from a comet hit Earth's atmosphere and burn up, they turn into multiple shooting stars. During the Perseids meteor shower, that occurs every year in July and August, it's possible to see 50 to 100 shooting stars per hour if the sky is clear.

COMETS ARE DIFFERENT FROM SHOOTING STARS. A COMET IS A BALL OF ICE AND ROCK THAT ORBITS THE SUN.

DO SHOOTING STARS EVER HIT THE GROUND?

Most shooting stars are made of small amounts of matter that burn up completely when they hit our atmosphere. When larger lumps pass through the atmosphere, they still heat up and create a trail, but they don't get completely burnt up and the remains land on Earth's surface. When these lumps hit the ground, they are known as meteorites.

IS AN ASTEROID A SHOOTING STAR?

No – an asteroid is a lump of rock that was left behind after the Solar System formed. Asteroids can be found throughout the Solar System, but many sit in the Asteroid Belt between Mars and Jupiter. Astronomers have currently identified over 1 million asteroids in our Solar System, but there may be millions more. These lumps vary in size – from titchy rocks that are about ten metres wide to mighty mounds that measure over 500 km across.

WHY IS GRAVITY DIFFERENT ON OTHER PLANETS?

Gravity is the force of attraction between objects that have mass. Anything with mass produces a gravitational force – from the Sun to Earth to you! However, the more massive an object is, the bigger its gravitational force. The planets in our Solar System all have different masses, and this means that the gravitational force you'd feel on each of them would vary.

 TIPPING THE SCALES

One way to measure this is by looking at how your weight would change if you stood on different planets. The bigger the planet's gravity, the more you'd weigh on its surface. This shows what you would weigh on the other planets in the Solar System if you weighed 22 kg on Earth:

Earth = 22 kg

Mercury = 8.3 kg

Mars = 8.3 kg

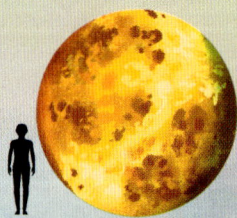
Venus = 20 kg

Uranus = 20.2 kg

Saturn = 20.5 kg

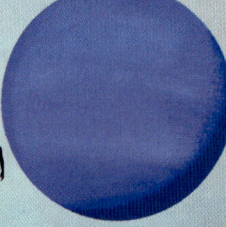
Neptune = 24.6 kg

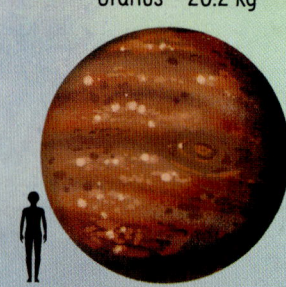
Jupiter = 51.5 kg

MIGHTY MARS

The fact that gravity varies between planets may just seem like a weird fact, but it could have implications in the future when people get to Mars.

Like Mercury, Mars is less massive than Earth – gravity on Mars' surface is around a third of what we experience here. Mars' smaller gravitational force would make a person used to Earth's gravity feel unusually strong. On Mars, you'd be able to jump higher and lift more massive things than you would on Earth.

WHY DOES IT MATTER?

Our bodies have developed to grow and thrive in Earth's gravity, so we don't know how they'd cope if they were exposed to Martian gravity for a long time. It's possible that our bones and muscles might weaken without the familiar pull of our home planet's gravity.

Scientists are currently investigating how medicines and exercises could combat the effects of low gravity in future human missions to Mars.

WHAT IS AN ECLIPSE?

Before you read any further, promise me you will NEVER look directly at the Sun or a solar eclipse. It will damage your eyesight forever. Promised? OK, read on …

An eclipse happens when a planet or moon blocks the light from the Sun. On Earth we see two main types of eclipse – lunar eclipses and solar eclipses.

LUNAR ECLIPSES

The Moon appears bright in our night sky, but it doesn't produce any light of its own. Instead, its surface reflects light from the Sun. During a lunar eclipse, Earth moves between the Moon and the Sun, blocking this light. You can look at a lunar eclipse safely using just your eyes.

SOLAR ECLIPSES

A solar eclipse happens when the Moon moves exactly between the Sun and the Earth, and casts it shadow on the Earth's surface. There are three kinds of solar eclipse that you can see from Earth. The only way to safely view any of them is through special solar glasses or by looking at a projection of the eclipse through a pinhole projector.

1.
PARTIAL SOLAR ECLIPSE

This is when the Sun, Moon and Earth are not completely aligned, so the Sun is only partially covered by the Moon.

2.
ANNULAR SOLAR ECLIPSE

This is when the Moon covers the central part of the Sun, but the outer edges are still visible.

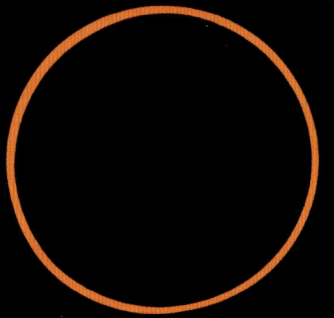

3.
TOTAL SOLAR ECLIPSE

This is the sort of eclipse that will blow your socks off! A total solar eclipse happens when the Moon sits at just the right distance from the Earth to completely cover the Sun. During a total solar eclipse, the sky goes dark and the only part of the Sun that remains visible is its outer atmosphere, called the corona.

CAN YOU SEE SOLAR ECLIPSES ON OTHER PLANETS?

Solar eclipses can be seen on other planets in our Solar System, but they aren't as jaw-dropping as those we experience on Earth. What makes our planet number one for eclipses is the size of our Moon. No other moon in the Solar System is so large compared to its parent planet, meaning that no other moon can block the Sun's light so completely and spectacularly as ours.

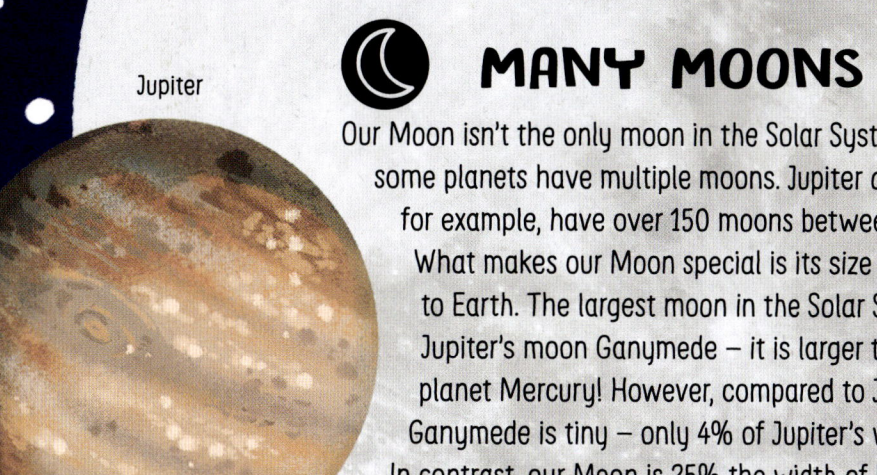

Jupiter

🌙 MANY MOONS

Our Moon isn't the only moon in the Solar System, and some planets have multiple moons. Jupiter and Saturn, for example, have over 150 moons between them. What makes our Moon special is its size compared to Earth. The largest moon in the Solar System is Jupiter's moon Ganymede – it is larger than the planet Mercury! However, compared to Jupiter, Ganymede is tiny – only 4% of Jupiter's width. In contrast, our Moon is 25% the width of Earth.

Ganymede

EXTRA-TERRESTRIAL ECLIPSES

A moon has to be the perfect size and the perfect distance between the Sun and its parent planet for it to block the Sun completely. Otherwise, eclipses on that planet won't be as incredible or as noticeable as those on Earth. Eclipses have been seen by rovers on Mars' surface but Mars' tiny moons just appear like shapes across the Sun.

Of course, these days we are finding planets orbiting stars far beyond our Solar System, so it's possible there are cosmic coincidences out there that produce something like those we're lucky enough to see on Earth.

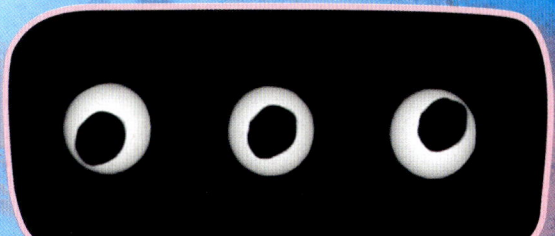

THIS SEQUENCE SHOWS MARS' LARGEST MOON, PHOBOS, PASSING IN FRONT OF THE SUN.

ARE THERE RAINBOWS ON OTHER PLANETS?

We don't know for certain if the right conditions exist on other planets to create rainbows. On Earth, rainbows are stunning natural spectacles created by sunlight passing through water. On a rainy day, when sunlight breaks through rain clouds or when sunlight passes through a waterfall, you might see a rainbow.

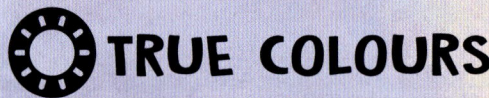

TRUE COLOURS

Sunlight is made up of lots of different 'waves' of light. These waves are usually all mixed up together to form 'white' light (for instance, normal daylight). However, when sunlight hits a drop of water, these waves separate.

This happens because the different waves of light travel at different speeds. When they pass through the raindrop they all slow down, but some slow down more than others. If the angle is correct, the waves separate as they emerge from the drop, so we see different colours in the sky – red, orange, yellow, green, blue, indigo and violet.

OTHERWORLDLY RAINBOWS

One of the most likely places for rainbows in our Solar System is Titan, a moon of Saturn. A robotic probe called Huygens landed on Titan in 2005 and discovered an atmosphere rich in methane, a gas which can fall as rain. Titan is a long way from the Sun, but if a beam of sunlight were to pass through the moon's atmosphere and hit a drop of liquid methane, it's possible that a rainbow could be formed. A rainbow on Titan would probably have an orangey hint to it, as Titan's sky is a murky orange-brown colour.

ANOTHER MOON OF SATURN, ENCELADUS, HAS GREAT JETS OF WATER VAPOUR ERUPTING FROM ITS SURFACE. IT'S POSSIBLE RAINBOWS COULD FORM THERE, TOO.

Try This At Home

You can make your own rainbow at home. All you need is a glass of water, a torch, a mirror and a dark room. Place the mirror into the glass so that it sits at an angle in the water. Shine the torch on to the mirror through one of the sides of the glass. You should be able to see a rainbow on the ceiling!

Since 1961, when the first human went into space, over 500 people from 41 countries have ventured out there. In this chapter, you can get the low-down on how we've explored space, what it takes to become an astronaut and what the future of our lives in space might look like.

WHAT HAPPENS DURING LIFT-OFF?

Imagine you are in a rocket just before lift-off. Apart from landing, this is the most dangerous part of your journey ... you're sitting on top of a huge explosion! But don't worry – it's a controlled explosion. When the fuel is lit, it will produce an enormous amount of exhaust gas. This gas will be funnelled through the rocket's nozzles to create a powerful pushing force – called thrust – which you need to get into space.

ROCKET FUEL

Rockets use either solid fuel or liquid fuel. When these fuels are mixed with oxygen and lit, they burn and create thrust.

The good thing about solid fuel is that it burns steadily and produces a lot of thrust. However, the speed at which this fuel burns can't be sped up, slowed down or stopped, so it is hard to control the amount of thrust.

Liquid fuel provides less thrust than solid fuel, but it can be controlled. This allows astronauts to regulate the speed of the rocket.

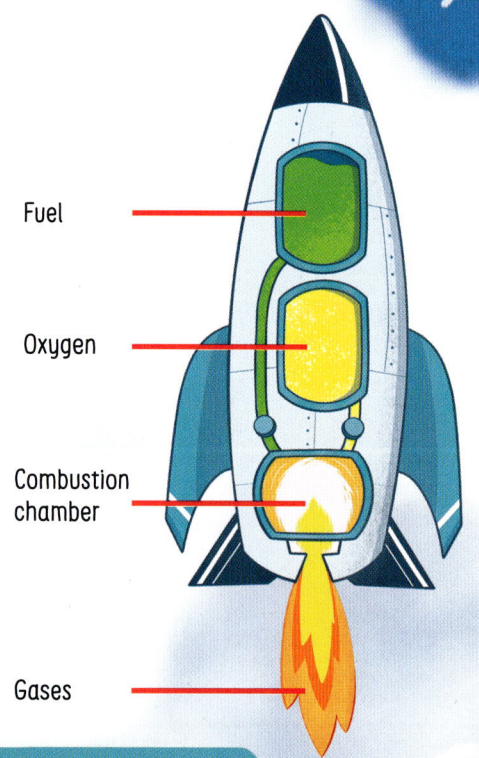

STRUCTURE OF A ROCKET

5, 4, 3, 2, 1 ...

The engines have been lit and the rocket is starting to rattle and shake. OOMPH! As the rocket moves up into the sky, you're pushed back in your seat by about three times your weight (the exact amount would depend on the size of the rocket). It's going faster and faster because, in order to escape Earth's gravity, the rocket needs to be travelling at a speed of at least 40,000 km per hour.

Finally, about ten minutes after lift-off, you suddenly go from feeling squished in your seat to feeling weightless.

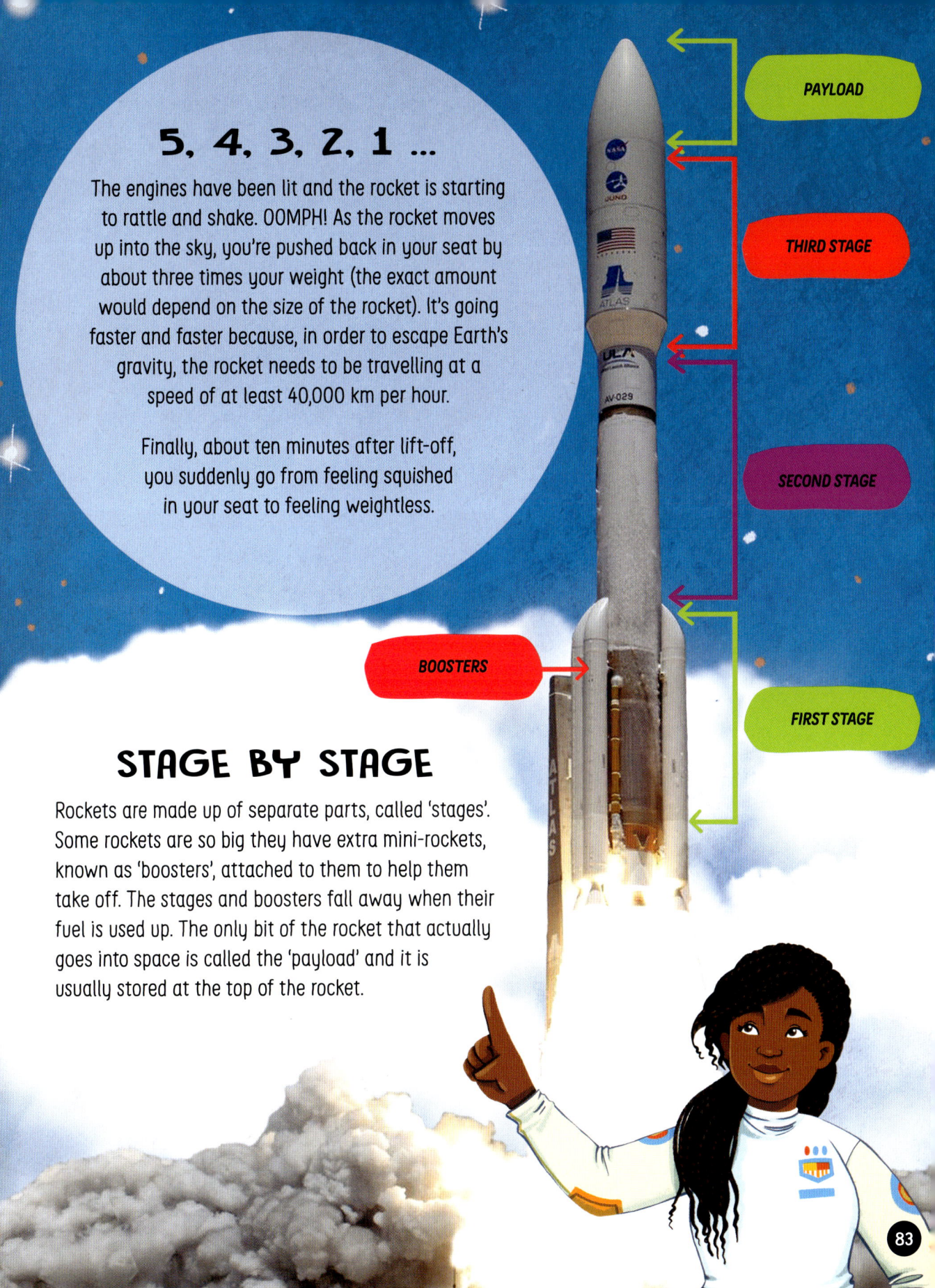

PAYLOAD

THIRD STAGE

SECOND STAGE

BOOSTERS

FIRST STAGE

STAGE BY STAGE

Rockets are made up of separate parts, called 'stages'. Some rockets are so big they have extra mini-rockets, known as 'boosters', attached to them to help them take off. The stages and boosters fall away when their fuel is used up. The only bit of the rocket that actually goes into space is called the 'payload' and it is usually stored at the top of the rocket.

WHY DO ASTRONAUTS FLOAT INSIDE SPACESHIPS?

You've probably seen videos of astronauts on the International Space Station (ISS) floating about in all directions. You might think this 'weightlessness' is to do with a lack of gravity, but that's not what's going on here – there isn't a point that you cross in space where you suddenly start floating. It is all to do with the special conditions that the astronauts are experiencing inside the spaceship as it orbits Earth.

GRAVITY'S PULL

It is true that an object's gravitational force gets weaker the further away you are from it. As we move further away from the centre of Earth, the planet's gravitational force isn't as strong. However, it is still there.

For example, there's a group of satellites called geostationary satellites orbiting Earth that sit around 35,000 km above the planet's surface. They're an incredibly long way away, but they stay in orbit because of the pull of Earth's gravity.

Astronauts on the ISS are only 400 km away from the surface of the Earth. Although there is a small reduction in gravity on the ISS, the astronauts still experience about 90% of the gravity that we feel down on the ground.

ASTRONAUT MAE JEMISON FLOATS AROUND ON THE ISS.

A LIFT EXPERIMENT

To understand what's going on, it might help to do a thought experiment.

Imagine you are in a lift in a very, very tall building. You get into the lift on the top floor and you start travelling down REALLY fast because the cables supporting the lift have broken. (Don't worry this is made up, and we've got thousands of cushions beneath us, so there will be a soft landing.)

If, while you and the lift are falling, you jump into the air, you are no longer touching the floor – you and the lift are falling at the same rate. A security person watching a camera showing the inside of the lift would see you floating above the lift floor. You'd seem weightless.

THE PHENOMENON IN WHICH PEOPLE AND OBJECTS APPEAR WEIGHTLESS IN SPACE IS KNOWN AS 'MICROGRAVITY'.

FREE-FALLING

Something similar would happen if you were an astronaut on the ISS. To be in orbit, your speed around Earth needs to be fast enough to balance the force of gravity that pulls you towards Earth. In this way, you are constantly falling, but your fall follows the curve of the Earth so you never land. This means that, just like in our thought experiment, both you and the ISS would be constantly falling towards the Earth and you'd feel weightless.

HOW DO ASTRONAUTS BREATHE INSIDE SPACESHIPS?

Take a breath in ... and out. You can do this thanks to Earth's atmosphere, a thin band of gas that surrounds our planet. We breathe in air which contains oxygen, and then we breathe out carbon dioxide. A spaceship is equipped with a system that recreates the oxygen levels found on Earth, so astronauts can breathe freely.

GOING UP!

The higher you go above Earth's surface, the thinner the atmosphere becomes. Mountain climbers find it hard to breathe up tall mountains, so they take supplies of oxygen with them. Astronauts travelling into space face the same problem. The difference is that a mountaineer on the top of Earth's tallest mountain, Everest, is about 9 km above sea level, so although the air is thin, it is still breathable. Astronauts go much, MUCH higher.

THE HIGH LIFE

Most astronauts travelling up through the atmosphere are heading for the International Space Station (ISS).

The ISS sits in low Earth orbit, around 400 km above the Earth's surface. The station is still in the Earth's atmosphere, but the air at this height is extremely thin.

To allow the astronauts on board to breathe, the station is kitted out with life-support systems. These refresh the air on the ISS, providing oxygen for the astronauts. A special machine called a 'scrubber' gets rid of gases such as carbon dioxide (CO_2), which are released when the astronauts breathe out and can be harmful in large amounts.

THE 'SCRUBBER' ON THE ISS

AIR LEAKS

Astronauts on board the ISS have to watch out for tiny leaks and block them to stop air escaping. Leaks can be caused by particles flying through space, which shoot through the layers of the spacecraft like bullets. The astronauts have a detector to track down the leaks, but sometimes they use creative methods! In 2020, a leak was found using tea leaves. The leaves were let loose in the air and pulled towards the minuscule crack.

WHY DO ASTRONAUTS WEAR SPACESUITS?

If you were to venture outside a spacecraft without a spacesuit, you wouldn't last long. The lack of air would mean that you wouldn't be able to breathe and the ice-cold temperatures would freeze you pretty quickly. A spacesuit provides an astronaut with everything they need to survive in space – essentially, it is like a mini spacecraft that you can wear.

MOST SPACESUITS ARE MADE UP OF SECTIONS THAT FIT TOGETHER TO FORM AN AIRTIGHT BARRIER. IT TAKES ABOUT 45 MINUTES TO PUT ONE ON!

SUITED AND BOOTED

There are two different types of spacesuit worn by astronauts. The first is a light-weight suit worn during take-off and landing. This provides oxygen for the astronaut just in case there are any problems with the air pressure inside the craft. The second is a white, bulky suit (see left) that is worn when the astronaut is outside the ship in space, taking part in a 'spacewalk'.

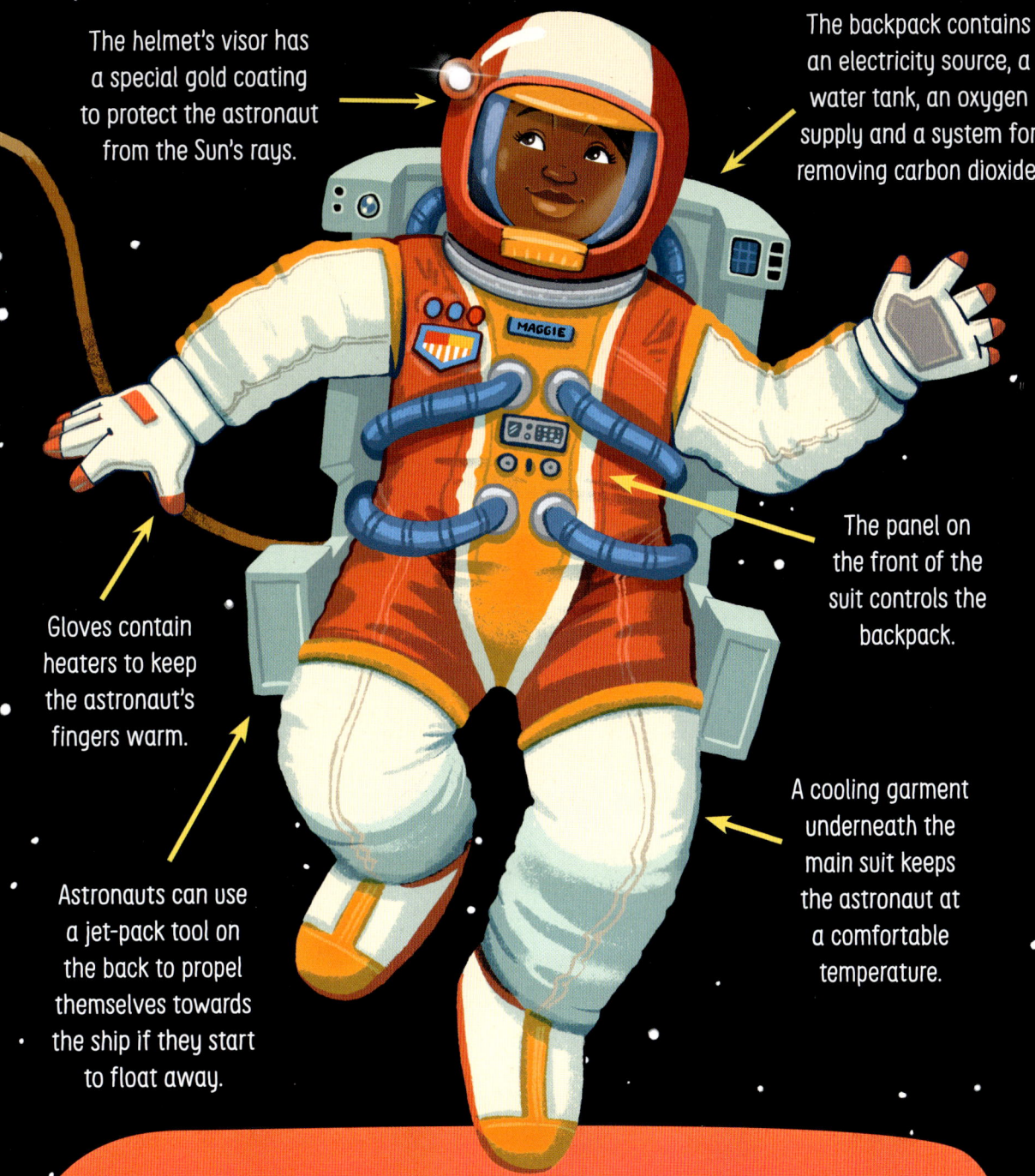

The helmet's visor has a special gold coating to protect the astronaut from the Sun's rays.

The backpack contains an electricity source, a water tank, an oxygen supply and a system for removing carbon dioxide.

Gloves contain heaters to keep the astronaut's fingers warm.

Astronauts can use a jet-pack tool on the back to propel themselves towards the ship if they start to float away.

The panel on the front of the suit controls the backpack.

A cooling garment underneath the main suit keeps the astronaut at a comfortable temperature.

SUITS YOU

The suit worn on spacewalks weighs around 130 kg, which is about as heavy as a baby elephant. Luckily, the astronauts don't feel the full weight due to microgravity. Although it's hefty, the suit is flexible enough to allow the astronaut to move around and carry out maintenance work outside the spacecraft. I've designed the suit above myself — in real-life, these suits look like the one on the opposite page.

89

WHAT DOES IT FEEL LIKE TO GO ON A SPACEWALK?

I once met the man who did the first ever spacewalk. He was a Russian cosmonaut called Alexei Leonov, who made his epic walk on the 18th March, 1965. He told me what he saw once he had made it out of his spacecraft – beautiful stars on one side, and glorious planet Earth on the other. He also noticed the deep silence of space once he was away from the noise of the spacecraft's engines.

FIRST STEPS

Everything went smoothly until Alexei finished his spacewalk and tried to get back into the spacecraft. He realized that in the vacuum of space his spacesuit had inflated! This had happened because of the big difference between the very low pressure in space and the much higher pressure in his suit. But Alexei kept a cool head. He let a little bit of air out of his suit – just enough to allow him to climb safely back inside the spacecraft.

ASTRO STROLL

Nowadays, astronauts have to do spacewalks regularly to carry out a variety of jobs – from maintaining a spacecraft to doing science experiments. Depending on the job, spacewalks can take only a few minutes or last for hours. The longest spacewalk to date took 8 hours and 56 minutes!

PRACTICE POOL

Astronauts spend a long time on Earth training for spacewalks, so they know exactly what to do. Training takes place in a facility called a Neutral Buoyancy Laboratory. This contains a very large pool with special equipment so astronauts can practise the sorts of tasks they'll need to do in space while feeling weightless.

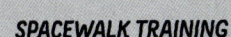

SPACEWALK TRAINING

WHAT DOES SPACE SMELL LIKE?

There is a saying that in space no one can hear you scream. Well, no one can smell you, either! We can't hear anything in space because it is a vacuum (an area without gas) and to hear sounds vibrations need to be carried by molecules, usually in a gas or liquid. The same goes for smell. In order to smell something, you need molecules of the substance to travel up your nose where special sensors will interact with the molecules and tell you what you're smelling.

RASPBERRIES AND RUM

Even if we cannot smell space directly, one of the things we can do is work out the chemical composition of molecules in different locations in space. From this, we can work out what these places may smell like.

In 2009, scientists were able to identify a chemical in a nebula at the centre of our Milky Way galaxy. This chemical is called ethyl formate and it appears on Earth, too. It's the chemical that gives raspberries their fruity flavour and it smells rather like rum. So, you could say that some parts of space smell like a pirate's favourite drink!

PLANET PONG

If we were able to take a whiff of the other planets in our Solar System, the smell that we are most likely to encounter seems to be, rather disappointingly, rotten eggs. This comes from a chemical called hydrogen sulphide, which occurs on the inner planets of the Solar System and in small amounts in the outer planets. If we could smell them, our neighbouring planets would be pretty stinky places!

SOME ASTRONAUTS SAY THAT THE INTERNATIONAL SPACE STATION SMELLS LIKE BURNING METAL AND BARBECUED MEAT.

QUICK QUESTIONS ON ...
LIFE ON THE ISS

HOW DO ASTRONAUTS SLEEP?

Astronauts don't lie in a bed like we do on Earth, as this would take up a lot of room and each astronaut would need to be tied to their mattress to stop them floating about. Instead, the crew on the International Space Station (ISS) have sleeping bags which they can zip themselves into. These bags are attached to the wall using Velcro, so the astronauts can snooze securely.

WHAT DO ASTRONAUTS EAT?

Astronauts used to eat flavoured paste or dehydrated food ... Yuck! Today, space meals are more like the sort of food you'd eat on a plane. Food is delivered to the ISS every 90 days, and includes fresh fruit and vegetables, chocolate bars and pre-packed meals. Meals are eaten with magnetic cutlery that sticks to the table. Drinks such as lemonade and juice are kept inside sealed packets and drunk with a straw, so the liquid doesn't fly around the station.

HOW DO ASTRONAUTS HAVE FUN?

To me, living in space has always sounded like a lot of fun. Astronauts work hard, but they also have free time – they can speak to their families back on Earth, play games with crewmates and even play music. One of the top pastimes on board the ISS is to look out of the window at Earth. With a sunrise and a sunset every 45 minutes, there's always something to see.

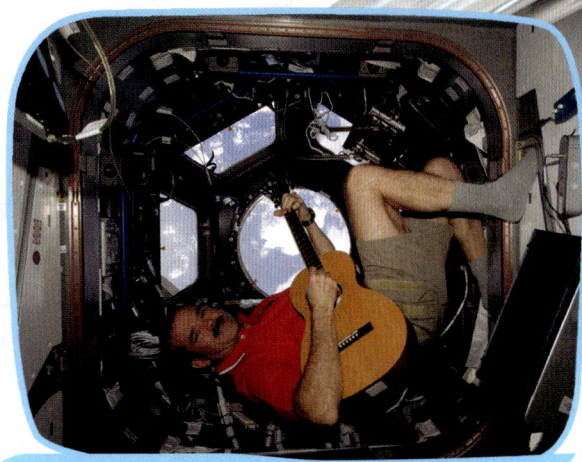

CANADIAN ASTRONAUT CHRIS HADFIELD TOOK HIS GUITAR TO THE ISS IN 2012.

CAN YOU HAVE A SHOWER AND GO TO THE LOO?

Water is expensive to get into space and doesn't behave like it does on Earth due to microgravity.

If you turned a shower on inside the ISS, the droplets would float around rather than fall to the floor. This could damage equipment so, instead, astronauts use no-rinse body washes and shampoo.

They also use a special toilet that sucks away poo and wee. Poo is sent back to Earth to be disposed of. Wee is recycled into water that's safe to drink. I've spoken to astronauts who say it tastes ... er ... fine!

NASA ASTRONAUT KAREN NYBERG DEMONSTRATES HOW WATER FLOATS IN MID-AIR ON THE ISS.

WHY DON'T WE LIVE ON OTHER PLANETS YET?

I've been asking this question for many years because I have wanted to travel to other planets all my life. Although there are currently a lot of technical hurdles that stop us from living on other planets, I think the biggest challenge we face is the cost of getting there and setting up a base with the complex systems needed to support human life on an alien planet.

NEW HOMES

If we could overcome the cost, where could we live? It's not a planet, but the nearest option is our Moon. It would be difficult to live there due to the lack of atmosphere, exposure to the Sun's radiation and the contrast between scorching temperatures (120 °C) on the day side and freezing temperatures (−130 °C) on the night side. But the Moon could act as a stepping stone between Earth and the rest of the Solar System. As the Moon is much less massive than Earth, it's easier to take off from its surface.

The other candidate is Mars. Living on Mars would have its challenges. Its temperatures are similar to those in Antarctica and it has a thin atmosphere that we can't breathe. However, water has been found on Mars, especially at its ice caps, and this would be crucial for human survival there.

ALIEN HOUSES

If we wanted to live on the Moon or Mars, we would need to build shelters to protect us from their environments. These could be similar to structures built in Antarctica (below), which allow scientists to live on the continent all year round, despite the extremely cold conditions.

These houses would need to provide a complete life-support system with a breathable atmosphere, protection from radiation, and a source of food, water and energy. Living on Mars would probably be very like living on board the International Space Station (pages 94–95). What do you think a Martian house would look like?

COULD WE GROW PLANTS ON OTHER PLANETS?

To make a home on another planet, we'd need to find a way to grow plants to feed ourselves, as transporting plants across space would be very expensive. Plants need light, water, air and the right temperature to grow. While Earth is a plant paradise, the same can't be said for the other planets in our Solar System. Out of them all, Mars is the best candidate. This is because its atmosphere is the most similar to Earth's. Turning the red planet into a green one would be hard, but not impossible.

PLANT PROBLEMS

Plants need particular things to grow that you don't find on Mars. Unlike Earth, Mars' atmosphere contains very high levels of carbon dioxide (CO_2) and very low levels of oxygen. Although plants do need CO_2 for photosynthesis, they also need oxygen to breathe — and there isn't enough oxygen for them to do this on Mars.

Mars also gets REALLY cold. At night, temperatures can drop to −99 °C, which would kill plants. Another problem is soil. Earth's soil is rich with chemicals and nutrients, mainly from dead plant matter, which help plants grow, but these things are missing from Mars' dusty surface.

MARTIAN KETCHUP

To survive on Mars, any plant would need to be grown in a greenhouse where we could control the temperature and amount of oxygen, and provide water. We would also need to add fertilizers to the Martian soil.

A recent experiment on Earth suggested that plants can grow and flourish in these conditions. Scientists created soil that mirrored Mars' dust. They popped this soil in a greenhouse with artificial lighting, added fertilizers and some specially chosen tomato seeds ... and the plants grew. In fact, the tomatoes were so successful, the scientists were able to make ketchup with them afterwards!

OVER A LONG PERIOD OF TIME, IT MIGHT EVEN BE POSSIBLE FOR PLANTS TO ADAPT AND GROW OUTSIDE ON MARS.

Try This At Home

You can do a simple experiment at home to see how plants grow in different types of soil. Take three plastic cups and make small drainage holes in their bases. Fill each cup with a different type of material – for instance, compost, ordinary soil and sand. Bury a seed (sunflower seeds work well) in each cup, place them on a sunny windowsill and water regularly. Which one grows the best?

COULD ANIMALS COME AND LIVE WITH US ON OTHER PLANETS?

Animals could certainly come and live with us on other planets – in fact, creatures such as monkeys, mice and cats all went into space long before humans did. If you love animals as much as space, then you probably can't imagine heading off to a new life on another world without your four-legged friends. But whether life in space would be much fun for your pets is another matter.

ANIMAL PIONEERS

The first animals to be sent into space were fruit flies, which were launched in a V2 rocket on 20th February, 1947, and the first animal to orbit Earth was a dog named Laika. She was sent up into space on board a Russian spacecraft, Sputnik 2, on 3rd November, 1957. Although they paved the way for successful animal space trips and, eventually, human journeys into space, many of these early animal voyages ended tragically.

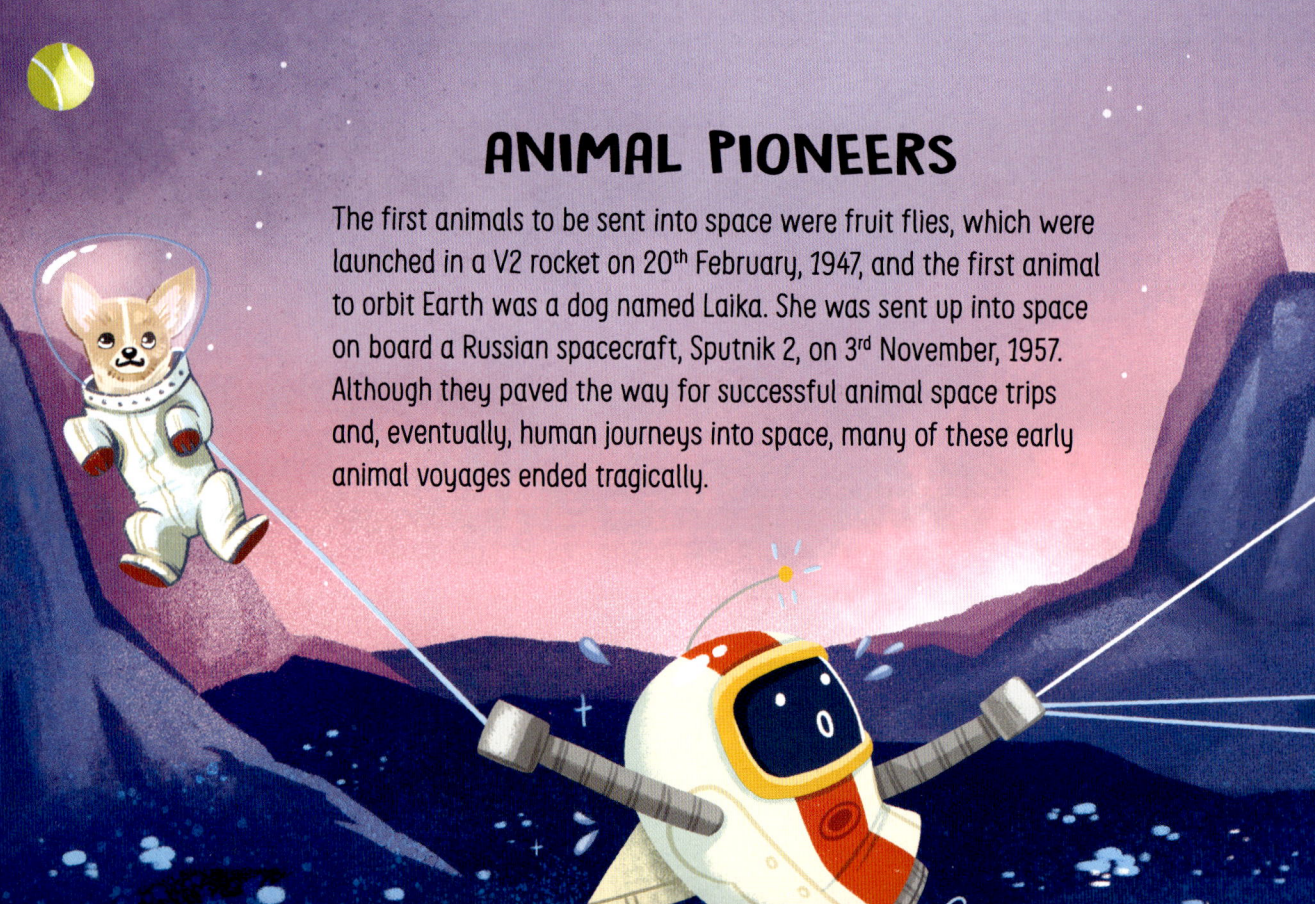

SPIDERS IN SPACE

Today, animals are only sent into space if it is absolutely necessary and they are looked after with care. Recent animal missions have resulted in some fascinating insights. In 2011, two golden orb spiders called Gladys and Esmeralda were sent to the International Space Station so scientists could study the effect of microgravity on their behaviour. Surprisingly, the spiders' webs looked much like those they'd spin on Earth, just a little rounder. And they were still lightning-quick at catching flies!

WALKIES ON MARS?

Just like humans, animals would be affected by the extreme conditions we'd encounter on other planets. For example, no animal would be able to breathe the atmosphere or survive the high levels of radiation found on Mars. And even penguins, adapted to cope with freezing Antarctic conditions, would find Mars extremely cold.

Any animal that made the journey to another planet alongside us would have to be confined to a shelter with life-support systems in order to survive. If you're planning a trip to Mars, Whiskers or Rex would probably be happier staying put on Earth.

COULD I SING IN SPACE?

You would be able to sing in space if you were somewhere with an atmosphere. However, your voice would sound very different depending on where you were and what gases were present in that atmosphere.

🎵 SPACE SOUNDS

To sing I need to take air into my lungs, then force that air over my vocal cords at the back of my throat. As the air passes over my vocal cords, they adjust to produce different sounds. When the air emerges from my mouth, these notes are carried by the air to whoever is close to me. So, in order to belt out my favourite tune, I need a gas or another medium (such as water) to carry the sounds.

Space is a vacuum, so there aren't any gases there. This means you wouldn't be able to sing if you were floating through space without a spacesuit. But if you were in a spacesuit, you would be able to sing, because spacesuits are filled with air to allow astronauts to breathe. The same goes for a spaceship – you'd be able to sing there as much as you like ... as long as your fellow passengers didn't mind!

WHAT ABOUT OTHER PLANETS?

If you've ever seen someone breathing in helium from a balloon and speaking, you'll know their voice sounds super squeaky. This happens because helium molecules are lighter than the nitrogen and oxygen molecules that largely make up air. Sound travels three times faster in a light gas, such as helium, than it does in nitrogen and oxygen, so it comes out at a more high-pitched frequency.

Something similar would happen if you tried to sing on other planets that have atmospheres which contain different gases to Earth's.

VENUS

Venus' atmosphere is mainly made up of carbon dioxide (CO_2). CO_2 is denser than air, so our vocal cords would react in the opposite way to how they do with helium. If you sang on Venus, your voice would sound deeper. At the same time, because Venus' atmosphere is thick – more like soup than air – the sound would travel faster, so you'd probably sound a bit like a duck.

MARS

Mars' atmosphere is much thinner than Earth's but, like Venus, it contains a lot of CO_2, so your singing voice would be a bit deeper. Even so, you wouldn't be able to make yourself heard as well as you can on Earth because Mars' thin atmosphere would not carry much sound – your voice would sound deeper but muffled.

COULD I USE MY PHONE IN SPACE?

This depends on the type of phone that you have. Most people have devices that are designed to connect to phone towers on Earth. These towers pick up phone signals in a local area – their average range is about 70 km. So if you were 400 km above Earth on the International Space Station (ISS) your normal phone definitely wouldn't work!

PHONE HOME?

There is a special type of phone called a satellite phone. These phones use satellites orbiting Earth, instead of Earth-based towers, to send information. If you were in a spaceship but in range of one of these satellites – as you would be on board the ISS – it's possible you'd be able to phone your friends and say, 'Hey, I'm in space!'

There are two types of satellite phone. The first use satellites in low Earth orbit (LEO) and the second use 'geostationary' satellites. Find out more opposite.

PEOPLE ON THE ISS DON'T USE NORMAL PHONES. INSTEAD, THEY HAVE A DIRECT LINK TO EARTH THROUGH A PRIVATE NETWORK THAT USES A MIX OF SATELLITES AND ANTENNAE.

1. LEO PHONES

LEO satellites sit 1,000 km above Earth and orbit the planet every 100 minutes. Just like a tower on Earth's surface, each satellite covers a limited area. To stop calls on Earth from cutting out when a satellite moves out of range, there's a system of around 70 satellites in low Earth orbit, which pass signals to one another. This would work in a similar way if you were making a call from the ISS. But because you'd be orbiting the Earth in the ISS alongside the satellites, your signal might drop in and out.

2. GEOSTATIONARY PHONES

Geostationary satellites also orbit Earth, but each orbit takes 24 hours – the same amount of time that Earth takes to rotate once on its axis. This means that these satellites are always above the same part of Earth and provide a stable signal.

In order to orbit the Earth in 24 hours, these satellites need to be a LONG way out – they sit 35,000 km above the Earth's surface. They have to be very powerful to pick up signals from Earth and it is expensive to use them for calls. You could phone home from the ISS with a geostationary phone – but your parents wouldn't be pleased as the bill would be MEGA!

HOW DO I BECOME AN ASTRONAUT?

Ever watched astronauts blasting off into space and thought 'I'd love to do that'? Astronauts train in special schools in various regions of the world – there may be one in or near your home country. Becoming an astronaut takes many years of hard work, even before your feet have left the ground. But if shooting for the stars is your dream, read on …

SPACE SCHOOL

The major astronaut-training programmes are led by Japan, India, Russia, the European Space Agency and NASA in the USA. Astronauts take classes in topics such as space-station systems, engineering, maths, survival skills and weightlessness. Getting on to an astronaut course is competitive. In 2017, 18,300 people applied to NASA's training programme and only 12 were selected.

SPECIAL SKILLS

In the early days of space travel, the people picked to be astronauts tended to have military backgrounds or experience of flying planes. The skills that are required for trainee astronauts today are a bit different:

- ✓ You should have a university degree in a relevant subject, such as maths, science, engineering or technology.

- ✓ You'd need to get work experience for two years in your subject area after finishing your degree.

- ✓ Student astronauts must pass tough physical tests, so you need to be fit and healthy.

- ✓ As well as carrying out scientific work and enduring difficult physical conditions on-board a spacecraft, you need to work well as part of a team.

- ✓ Knowing some basic Russian is also a plus. The two main languages spoken on the ISS are English and Russian.

ASTRONAUT SUNITA WILLIAMS IN TRAINING

Astro Fact

As well as national space programmes, there are new opportunities to become an astronaut with private companies, such as SpaceX, Blue Origin and Virgin Galactic, that take paying customers into space. In the future, I think that more and more of us will have the opportunity to go into space. See you up there!

QUICK QUESTIONS ON ...
SPACE RECORDS

WHO WAS THE FIRST PERSON TO GO INTO SPACE?

The first person to travel into space was Yuri Gagarin. He was a Russian pilot who trained to be a cosmonaut (the Russian word for astronaut). Gagarin was 27 years old when he went into space on his own on the 12th April, 1961. As he blasted off, Gagarin said 'Poyekhali!', which means 'Let's go!' in Russian. Gagarin spent 1 hour and 29 minutes in space and orbited the Earth once.

WHAT'S THE WEIRDEST THING THAT'S BEEN SENT INTO SPACE?

I think two of the weirdest things that have gone into space are a mini harmonica and a set of tiny bells.

On 16th December, 1965, astronauts on the Gemini 6A mission decided to play a Christmas joke on mission control. They reported seeing a 'satellite going from north to south', driven by a pilot 'wearing a red suit'.

After this message, the astronauts took out the instruments and performed 'Jingle Bells'. The harmonica and bells were the first musical instruments to be played in space.

WHAT WAS THE FIRST SATELLITE?

The first satellite was launched on 4th October, 1957. It was called 'Sputnik', which means 'fellow traveller' in Russian. It was made by the Soviet Union and was the first human-made object to go into space. Sputnik also marked the start of the 'Space Race', a period during the 20th century when the USA and the Soviet Union competed to explore space.

SPUTNIK 1

HOW MANY PEOPLE HAVE BEEN INTO SPACE?

The number currently stands at around 600, but it is going up all the time. Until recently, it was easy to keep track of how many people had been into space, as the numbers increased slowly with each human-led mission. However, with the development of space tourist companies, the numbers may start to go up a lot quicker. Maybe you will be one of them!

DID A PERSON DRIVE A CAR ON THE MOON?

It sounds crazy but yes, people have driven around on the Moon – not just once, but three times! You might be picturing an astronaut zipping around craters in something that looks very similar to your family car, but the vehicles used on the Moon looked more like golf buggies. Nicknamed 'Moon buggies', these cars were officially called Lunar Roving Vehicles.

TEST DRIVE

The buggies were sent to the Moon as part of the Apollo space program. The first Moon landing happened on the 20th July, 1969, when two Apollo 11 astronauts, Neil Armstrong and Buzz Aldrin, walked about on the Moon's surface. However, it wasn't until 1971 that the first Moon buggy landed, as part of the Apollo 15 mission.

ONE OF THE BUGGIES PARKED ON THE MOON

BRILLIANT BUGGIES

The Moon buggies were designed to carry the astronauts further than they could walk on foot, so they could analyse more of the Moon's surface. Between them, the three buggies covered a distance of just under 100 km. At the end of the missions, the Moon buggies were left on the surface and still sit there to this day.

CAMERAS WERE ATTACHED TO THE BUGGIES SO THE VEHICLES COULD RECORD THE ASTRONAUTS BLASTING OFF FROM THE MOON AT THE END OF THEIR MISSIONS.

FANCY A SPIN?

Since the Apollo 17 mission in 1972, no person has set foot on the Moon. That may be about to change. A new NASA mission called Artemis is planning to return people to the Moon's surface — it will land people of different ethnic backgrounds and the first woman on the Moon by 2025 or 2026. If you ever get a chance to visit the Moon, be sure to take a Moon buggy for a spin.

HOW FAR CAN SPACE TELESCOPES SEE?

With an amateur telescope, you can see surprisingly far into space – you can spot stars and nebulae that are thousands of light years away. But this question is about another level of telescope – the telescopes that we have sent up into space. These super scopes can peer outward for BILLIONS of light years.

Since 1990, the biggest and most revolutionary space telescope has been the Hubble. Named after the astronomer Edwin Hubble, the telescope was launched into orbit 570 km above Earth. Its position means that Hubble has been easily maintained and updated by astronauts. Over the years, Hubble has made over 1.5 million observations and has studied locations more than 13.4 billion light years from Earth.

The James Webb Telescope launched in 2021 and is the most advanced space telescope to date. While Hubble looks at things in visible light (the things we can see with our eyes) and ultraviolet light, James Webb studies the Universe by detecting infrared light or heat energy. This means it can see different things to Hubble and look at objects in very distant galaxies. It can also peer back even further in time.

A PHOTO TAKEN BY HUBBLE CAPTURES DRAMATIC PILLARS OF DUST AND GAS INSIDE A NEBULA.

WHAT'S THE FURTHEST OBJECT FROM EARTH THAT A SPACECRAFT HAS LANDED ON?

On 14th January, 2005, a robotic space probe called Huygens touched down on Titan, one of Saturn's moons. Titan is located about 1 billion km from Earth. Huygens was the first human-made object to land on a world in the outer Solar System.

Buffeted by winds as it dropped through Titan's atmosphere, Huygens collected recordings and photos of the moon during its 2.5 hour fall to the surface.

When it landed, the probe took pictures of Titan's surface for another hour before communication was lost. The data that Huygens sent back revealed that Titan was home to lakes and rivers of liquid methane.

Huygens travelled to Saturn's moon on a craft called Cassini, as part of a joint mission between NASA and the European Space Agency. It took this intrepid spacecraft over six years to reach its destination. Cassini went into orbit around Saturn and analysed the planet for over 13 years. This ground-breaking mission allowed scientists back home to study the planet's magnetic field and its rings up close.

A CLOSE-UP OF SATURN TAKEN BY CASSINI

WILL EVERYONE BE TRAVELLING INTO SPACE 100 YEARS FROM NOW?

Up until recently, the only people to go into space were astronauts working on missions led by space agencies. The development of new 'space tourism' companies is changing this. I think in the next 100 years many more of us will be travelling out to orbit Earth – and maybe even making it as far as the Moon, or even Mars.

TAKING FLIGHT

We take it for granted now, but even jetting off to other parts of our home planet is something we've only been able to do for the last 100 years. The first commercial flight took place on 1st January, 1914. Fast forward to 2019, and 4.5 billion people were taking flights around the world every year.

BLAST OFF

Space tourism is in a similar place now to where plane travel was in 1914, with companies keen to respond to people's desire to experience the thrill of space. On 15th September, 2021, the first all-civilian spaceflight lifted off as part of the Inspiration4 mission. The four people on board spent three days orbiting Earth before being brought back down to land (with a splash!) in the Atlantic Ocean.

REACH FOR THE STARS

Reaching for the stars is a dream come true, but there are challenges to be met. Just like planes, rockets have a significant impact on the environment. Getting into space is also jaw-droppingly expensive – the Inspiration4 mission was paid for by a billionaire. Before we start jetting off into the cosmos, I think making sure space travel is environmentally friendly and accessible to everyone should be our number-one priority for the next 100 years.

GLOSSARY

Here are explanations of some handy space and science words.

asteroid
A chunk of rock and metal that orbits the Sun.

atmosphere
A layer of gases that surrounds a planet.

atoms
Tiny particles that make up everything that surrounds us.

aurora
A display of light caused by particles from the Sun hitting a planet's magnetic field.

axis of rotation
An imaginary line that an object, such as a planet, rotates around.

carbon
An element that exists in all plants and animals, and is found in diamonds and coal.

carbon dioxide (CO_2)
A colourless, odourless gas made up of the elements carbon and oxygen.

conductor
A material that heat, electricity or sound can flow through.

constellation
A group of stars that appears in a certain formation and has a name, such as Orion.

core
The innermost part of a planet.

crust
The outermost part of a planet.

dark energy
The mysterious energy that is making the Universe expand.

dark matter
The invisible stuff in space that has gravity but is unlike regular matter.

density
A measurement that compares the amount of mass an object has to its volume.

eclipse
When one object in space blocks the view of another. For instance, during a lunar eclipse, Earth comes between the Sun and the Moon.

element
A substance made up of one type of atom. An element cannot be split into other substances. Elements are the building blocks of all matter.

exoplanet
A planet that orbits a star outside our Solar System.

friction
The force of resistance that one object or surface encounters when moving over another.

fusion
The process of joining atoms together, which produces different elements and energy.

galaxy
A group of stars, planets and other bodies held together by gravity.

gravity
A force of attraction between all things with mass.

greenhouse gas
A gas in a planet's atmosphere that traps heat. On Earth, greenhouse gases include methane and carbon dioxide.

hydrogen
A colourless, odourless gas. It is the simplest, lightest and most common element in the Universe.

infrared light
A type of radiated energy that humans cannot see but can feel as heat.

light pollution
The presence of light, which can make it harder to see starlight at night.

light year
A unit of length in space. It is the distance that light travels in a year, approximately 10 trillion km.

magnetic field
The volume around a magnetic object in which the magnetic forces due to the object can be felt.

mantle
The layer of a rocky planet or body which lies underneath the crust but above the core.

mass
The measure of how much matter there is in an object.

matter
Any object or substance that takes up space. Solid, liquid, gas and plasma are the four states of matter.

meteor
A small rock travelling through Earth's atmosphere. If it reaches Earth's surface, it is a 'meteorite'.

methane
A colourless, odourless gas made of molecules containing hydrogen and carbon. It is a greenhouse gas.

microgravity
Microgravity is a condition that exists when things are in a state of free fall. In a spacecraft, things appear to be weightless due to microgravity.

Milky Way
The galaxy in which our Solar System exists.

molecule
A group of atoms bonded together.

moon
A body that orbits around another planet or other body. Some asteroids have moons.

nebula
A cloud of gases and dust in outer space. Some nebulae are formed when a dying star explodes. Others are regions where new stars form.

orbit
The path of an object around a planet, star or moon.

oxygen
A colourless, odourless gas, which forms about 20% of the air on Earth and is essential for life.

photosynthesis
The process in which green plants use sunlight, water and carbon dioxide to make energy.

radiation
Energy, such as heat, that comes from a particular source.

retrorocket
A type of rocket engine that fires in the direction of travel to slow a craft down.

rover
A vehicle designed to explore the surface of a planet or moon.

satellite
A natural body (such as a moon) or a spacecraft that orbits another body.

skycrane
A mechanism that can be used to lower a lander from a retrorocket to the surface of a planet.

space probe
A robotic spacecraft launched into space to collect data that can be sent back to Earth.

thrust
A force that makes an object move.

water vapour
Water in the form of gas.

INDEX

Aldrin, Buzz 110
aliens 27, 28–29
animals 4, 28–29, 100–101
Antarctica 40, 48, 97, 101
Apollo program 110–111
Armstrong, Neil 110
Artemis mission 111
Asteroid Belt, the 69, 71
asteroids 17, 34, 36, 63, 71
astronauts 81, 82, 84–85, 86–87, 88–89, 90–91, 93, 94–95, 102, 106–107, 108, 110–111, 112, 114
auroras 65

Betelgeuse 37
Big Bang, the 5, 8–11, 32
Big Crunch, the 32, 33
Big Freeze, the 33
Big Rip, the 33
black holes 4, 5, 6, 18–21
Blue Origin 107
brown dwarfs 16

carbon 14, 39, 58–59, 67
carbon dioxide 41, 87, 89, 98, 103
Cassini-Huygens probe 63, 79, 113
Cepheid variables 8
comets 36, 56–57, 63, 70
corona, the 38, 75

dark energy 33
dark matter 32
diamonds 58–59
dwarf planets 34, 36, 68–69
 Ceres 69

Eris 69
Haumea 69
Makemake 69
Pluto 68–69

Earth 6, 9, 10–11, 13, 21, 22–23, 24–25, 26–27, 28–29, 30, 36–37, 38–39, 40–41, 42–43, 45, 46–47, 48–49, 50–51, 54, 58–59, 60–61, 62, 64–65, 69, 70–71, 72–73, 74–75, 76–77, 78, 83, 84–85, 86–87, 90–91, 92, 94–95, 97, 98–99, 100–101, 103, 104–105, 108, 112, 113, 114–115
eclipses 74–75, 76–77
 lunar eclipses 74
 solar eclipses 74–75, 76–77
European Space Agency, the 106, 113
event horizon, the 20
exoplanets 25, 26–27

fusion 12, 14–15, 16, 19

Gagarin, Yuri 108
Gaia 26
galaxies 6, 8–9, 18, 26–27, 30–31, 33, 92, 112
 Andromeda galaxy, the 31
 Milky Way, the 18, 26–27, 30–31, 92
Galilei, Galileo 63
Gemini 6A mission 108
global warming 41
gold 15, 89

gravity 12, 15, 17, 18–19, 20–21, 32–33, 45, 48–49, 52–53, 56–57, 63, 72–73, 83, 84–85, 89, 95
Great Red Spot, the 60–61

Hadfield, Chris 95
helium 14, 22, 67, 103
Hubble Space Telescope, the 112
Hubble, Edwin 8–9, 31, 32, 112
hydrogen 14, 22, 59, 67, 93

Inspiration4 115
International Space Station (ISS), the 13, 84–85, 87, 93, 94–95, 97, 101, 104–105, 107
iron 14

James Webb Telescope, the 23 112
Jemison, Mae 84
Jupiter 42–43, 44, 58–59, 60–61, 69, 71, 72, 77

Kuiper Belt, the 69

Laika 100
Leavitt, Henrietta 31
Leonov, Alexei 90
light years 10–11, 21, 22–23, 31, 112

magnetic fields 44, 65, 113
Mars 24–25, 42–43, 50–51, 52–53, 54–55, 69, 71, 72–73, 77, 97, 98–99, 101, 103, 114
Mercury 40–41, 42–43, 44, 72–73, 77
meteorites 71

meteors 70
methane 59, 67, 79, 113
microgravity 85, 89, 95, 101
Moon, the 43, 45, 46–47, 68, 74–75, 76–77, 97, 110–111, 114
Moon buggies 110–111
moons 26, 29, 34, 36, 44–45, 54, 63, 74, 76–77, 79, 86, 113
   Enceladus (moon of Saturn) 79
   Ganymede (moon of Jupiter) 44, 77
   Phobos (moon of Mars) 77
   Titan (moon of Saturn) 79, 113

NASA 33, 38, 48, 54–55, 95, 106, 111, 113
nebulae 5, 6, 12, 22–23, 92, 112
   Helix nebula, the 23
   Tarantula nebula, the 22
Neptune 42, 56, 66–67, 68, 69, 72
nitrogen 103
Nyberg, Karen 95

observable Universe, the 10–11
orbits 16, 19, 24–25, 26–27, 29, 34, 42–43, 44, 56–57, 62–63, 64–65, 68, 70, 77, 84–85, 87, 100, 104–105, 108, 112–113, 114–115
Orion constellation 37
oxygen 14, 29, 82, 86–87, 88–89, 98–99, 103

Parker probe 38–39
Parker, Eugene 38
Perseids, the 70
Philae probe 56–57

planetary nebulae 23
plants 28, 98–99
Pritchett, Carr Waller 61

radiation 10, 16, 19, 50, 57, 97, 101
rainbows 78–79
Rees, Sir Martin 21
retrorockets 53
rockets 13, 82–83, 100, 115
rovers 51, 52–53, 54–55, 77
   Curiosity 55
   Opportunity 54
   Perseverance 51, 52–53, 55
   Sojourner 54
   Spirit 54
   Zhurong 55

satellites 84, 104–105, 109
   Sputnik 1 109
   Sputnik 2 100

Saturn 42–43, 59, 62–63, 67, 72, 77, 79, 113
Schwabe, Samuel Heinrich 61
seasons 47, 64
shooting stars 70–71
silicon 14
silver 15
skycranes 53
Solar System, the 5, 24–25, 26, 34, 36, 40, 43, 44, 56–57, 60, 63, 64, 66–67, 68–69, 71, 72, 76–77, 79, 93, 97, 98, 113
Space Race, the 109
spacesuits 57, 88–89, 90, 102

spacewalks 88–89, 90–91
SpaceX 107
spaghettification 21
stardust 14
stars 6, 8–9, 12–13, 14–15, 16, 19, 22–23, 24–25, 26–27, 29, 30–31, 33, 34, 37, 43, 48, 68, 70, 77, 90, 112
   Proxima Centauri 13
stellar nurseries 23
Sun, the 12–13, 18, 21, 23, 24, 29, 34, 36–37, 38–39, 40, 42–43, 44, 46–47, 50, 56–57, 64–65, 66, 70, 72, 74–75, 76–77, 79, 89, 97
supernova 15

telescopes 8, 22–23, 31, 33, 42, 50, 61, 63, 112
Truth, Sojourner 54
Universe, the 4, 5, 6, 8–9, 10–11, 14, 27, 28–29, 31, 32–33, 112
Uranus 42, 64–65, 72

Venus 24, 40–41, 42–43, 64, 72, 103
Virgin Galactic 107, 109
Voyager 2 66–67

water 15, 25, 26, 29, 51, 54, 57, 78–79, 89, 95, 97, 98–99, 102
weightlessness 83, 84–85, 91, 106
Williams, Sunita 107

PICTURE CREDITS

Images taken from Shutterstock (www.shutterstock.com) apart from the following:

Page 10, bottom-left image: NASA/WMAP Science Team
Page 15, top-right image: NASA/Chandra X-ray Observatory Center
Page 19, background image: NASA Goddard; bottom-right image: NASA/JPL-Caltech
Page 23: NASA/JPL-Caltech/University of Arizona
Page 31, bottom-right image: David (Deddy) Dayag/Wikimedia Commons
Page 37, top-right image: Rogelio Bernal Andreo; bottom-right image: NASA
Page 38–39: NASA/Johns Hopkins APL/Steve Gribben
Page 48, bottom-left image: NASA
Page 51, bottom-right image: NASA/JPL-Caltech
Page 54, top-left image: NASA/JPL; bottom-left image: NASA/JPL-CALTECH/CORNELL/USGS
Page 55, top-right image: NASA/JPL-Caltech/MSSS; middle image: NASA/JPL-Caltech/University of Arizona; bottom-right image: Ingenuity on Mars, credit: NASA
Page 60, bottom-left image: enhanced image by Gerald Eichstadt and Sean Doran (CC BY-NC-SA) based on images provided courtesy of NASA/JPL-Caltech/SwRI/MSSS
Page 61: NASA/JPL-Caltech/SwRI/MSSS
Page 65, bottom-right image: NASA Goddard
Page 66–67: NASA/JPL
Page 68, bottom-left image: NASA/Johns Hopkins University Applied Physics Laboratory/Southwest Research Institute
Page 75, top-right image: NASA/Bill Ingalls
Page 83: NASA/Bill Ingalls
Page 84: NASA/Mae Jemison
Page 87: NASA/Anne McClain
Page 90–91, main image: NASA; bottom-right image: NASA/Josh Valcarcel
Page 95, top-right image: NASA; bottom-right image: NASA
Page 97, bottom-right image: Wikimedia Commons
Page 107, top-right image: NASA/James Blair
Page 110, bottom-left image: NASA
Page 111: NASA
Page 112, bottom-left image: NASA/ESA/STScI
Page 113, bottom-right image: NASA/JPL-Caltech/Space Science Institute

Every reasonable effort has been made to credit these images accurately. Any errors or omissions that may have occurred are inadvertent, and anyone with any queries is invited to write to the publishers, so that amendments may be included in subsequent editions of this work.